John Harms is a writer and broadcaster. His previous books include *Loose Men Everywhere* and *Play On*. He is a regular contributor to the *Age* and can be heard on ABC radio throughout the country.

Other books by John Harms

Confessions of a Thirteenth Man
Memoirs of a Mug Punter
Loose Men Everywhere
Play On (an omnibus of John Harms' first three books)

John
Harms

the
PEARL
STEVE RENOUF'S STORY

UQP

This book contains the names and photographs of Indigenous people who have passed away. The author wishes to remind the readers that this may cause them some distress or harm.

First published 2005 by University of Queensland Press
PO Box 6042, St Lucia, Queensland, 4067 Australia
Reprinted 2005

www.uqp.uq.edu.au

Typeset in 12.5/16.5 pt Bembo by Post Pre-press Group, Brisbane
Printed in Australia by McPherson's Printing Group

Distributed in the USA and Canada by
International Specialized Books Services, Inc.,
5824 N.E. Hassalo Street, Portland, Oregon 97213-3640

Cataloguing in Publication Data
National Library of Australia

Harms, John, 1962– .
 The Pearl: Steve Renouf's story.

 1. Renouf, Steve. 2. Rugby League football players - Queensland -
 Biography. 3. Athletes, Aboriginal Australian - Queensland - Biography.
 I. Title.

796.3338092

ISBN 0 7022 3536 9.

To all those who have encouraged and supported me, especially my Mum and Dad, Lis, Wayne Bennett and my Broncos teammates.

S. R.

To all those Indigenous footballers, who have given us so much joy over the years.

J. H.

Contents

Introduction

IT IS A BEAUTIFUL early morning in Brisbane in October 2002: one of those mornings which tell you the warmth is back in the sunshine. I drive my Veedub along Petrie Terrace, past the cranes busily reassembling Lang Park. I wonder whether the new boutique stadium will have the character of the old – and whether a mercurial player like Steve Renouf will ever be seen there again.

I drive along Newmarket Road, on through the suburbs, past thousands of homes where Queenslanders have leapt from their Jason recliners as Steve has sliced through another defence. No one moves like Steve Renouf. Past the West Mitchelton Rugby League Club. On to Samford Valley. Eventually I arrive at the entrance of the Renoufs' property in the foothills of Mt Glorious.

I wind up and down and around, and think what a job it must be to keep the long driveway in good nick. Past the dam. Past Nipper the pony, Freda the fresian and Holly the heifer. Up the rise. Past Claudia the camel. Through the gate to the house paddock. And park under the big Queensland nut tree – as Steve likes to call it. The Renoufs' magnificent Queenslander sits on the saddle of a hill overlooking the valley. It is a simple old farmhouse made grand by extension and renovation. It has lost none of its rural charm.

Steve comes out to greet me. 'G'day.' He is as fit as ever. And all smiles. He seems too gentle to have been a professional footballer, too easygoing or something. He's going to take me back to his home town. 'I've got the kids in the car already,' he says. 'Saves rounding them up.' I say g'day to Sam and Billy and Sunny who are strapped in and set to go. It's school holidays and they can't wait to see their cousins.

The goats gather around, and a few guineafowl scamper past. The dogs bound out to have a look. Steve's wife, Elissa, comes down from the house. She is lithe and bright. She looks like she's just stepped out of her high school photo. She carries Freddie, still a toddler, and Charlie, their second youngest, is at her feet. We chat for a while. She gives the entourage a few last-minute instructions and a bag of goodies, and Steve and I get into the four-wheel drive. We're away: off to Murgon.

We head over the mountain. The distinctive smell of the rainforest fills the car. Past Wivenhoe Dam. Over bridges named after local families. Through cattle country. The kids ask for chips and Dad says they can have a muesli bar or an apple. Lively Billy, who is eight, taunts his older brother, Sam. Sunny sits quietly, half admiring her older brothers and half shaking her head at them. She is learning resilience.

We stop at the servo at Moore. Steve takes out his insulin bag. He wonders out loud, as he sometimes does, 'Should I have a shot now?' He has diabetes, which he controls with insulin four times daily. He decides he will. He clicks the top of the pencil-like injector which punctures his leg. 'You hardly feel it,' he says.

We travel through timber country. We talk football. It is

NRL Grand Final week. The Broncos have been beaten by the Roosters in the preliminary final in Sydney. Steve was on the sidelines doing special comments for the Triple M radio station in Brisbane. 'Locky kept them in it in the first half, and then they had their chances. I don't know: there was just something missing.' It doesn't seem to trouble him too much. He's not like the diehard fan broken by another disappointment. He is confident that the Roosters will knock over the Warriors.

I ask him how Triple M's *Blood, Sweat and Beers* is going, the Saturday morning sports show on which Steve appears regularly. 'Yeah, pretty good.' It's a standard reply from Steve. I ask him about his long-term prospects as a commentator and he says he is waiting to hear more. We laugh that that's always the case in radio. Steve has enjoyed his media work during the year. I ask him about his new job with the Queensland Government's Department of Sport and Recreation. 'It's good,' he says. 'There's plenty happening, and a lot to learn.'

We pass trucks laden with pine logs, and wind our way into Blackbutt, the first of the towns of the South Burnett. There's something happening in the back seat. It's a conspiracy of children – giggling behind their hands but not saying anything. We turn right at the war memorial and find the football field. It's like walking back into the 1950s. The ancient lights would struggle to pierce the evening mist. There is a time-keeper's box and a big clock, and a white scoreboard and a couple of weathered advertising hoardings. The posts slant crazily, but somehow their angle matches the slope of the ground. You can almost hear the guttural roars of timbermen wearing the brown and green – front-rowers with axemen's hands – and the thud of bodies bashing together.

Steve looks at it all. There is life in his face. Memory. 'This was a dreaded trip,' he laughs. 'We called this "the cow paddock".'

We drive off and the kids are still giggling. On the outskirts of the town Sam finally plucks up the courage: 'We're in Blackbutt because Dad's got one. Get it?' We all laugh, Steve a little sheepishly at first. It's a family joke. Someone says it every time they're passing through – which is quite often. They love to visit family in Murgon. I wonder whether Sam thinks he's got a black butt as well.

In ten minutes we're in Yarraman. It looks like it's good grazing country. You can see the smoke stacks of the Tarong Power Station in the distance. And then on to Nanango. The sign tells us that the town was established in 1848. Lots of German settlers. We stop at the Fred Kassulke Oval, home of the Nanango Stags who wear the blue and white just like the old Fortitude Valley teams. 'They had big kids down here,' says Steve, chuckling. 'Workers coming and going. Stacks of Kiwis. Huge they were.'

The Stags' clubhouse is typically small-town Queensland: a basic weatherboard structure on two-foot-high stumps which, if it were in another location, could be a family home or the golf clubhouse or the office for an old petrol depot. A few wooden forms line the fence and you can imagine the ground ringed by cars, nose-in, tooting their horns for another Nanango try. Everyone from the district would be there, the young fellas in footy shorts with a beer in their hand.

We head into farming territory: the red, red, volcanic soil surrounding Kingaroy. Peanut country. Joh country. Peanut Joh country, in fact. And then into the bustling town of Kingaroy with its peanut silos which West Indian fast bowler Wes Hall famously threw a cricket ball over – or at least onto. There is a feeling that this is the big smoke, the hub of the South Burnett, with car dealerships and engineering works, fertiliser merchants and home-delivered pizza. Clearly, there are some wealthy people in this community.

The kids want Kentucky Fried. They are placated with a mini-packet of chips each that Mum has packed. We find the home-ground of the Kingaroy Red Ants. 'Silvertails,' says Steve, laughing, but you can tell he's serious. 'This is the headquarters of rugby league out this way – not that we liked to admit that.' There are dressing sheds and an allocated drinking area – the pigpen, where there were always plenty of laughs and the occasional barney.

We keep going towards Wondai, Steve telling stories of people from the area, like his mate Zombi Sempf, a second rower who played under-age representative footy for Wide Bay. And Darryl 'Dodo' Harrison, a brilliant young Aboriginal player who could have been anything, but didn't stick at it.

Aerialled utes flash the other way. They look like bull-terriers on tyres. They are shrines to Bundy, and have stickers which make mothers (and fathers) nervous. We pass a billboard that has been painted with more enthusiasm than skill, which advertises the local radio station: 'CROW FM – JUST LISTEN'. So we do. The kids are getting restless and Steve plays the firm hand with Billy. I smile. He winks at me. He's a good actor – and a good dad.

We drive through Wooroolin: a town of a few houses, a shop and the Grand Hotel, one of those classic watering holes where the publican throws you the keys and asks you to lock up when you've had enough; the sort of pub that could be chosen for a Fourex ad. Through Tingoora where Steve's grandmother lived for a while. And on to Wondai.

In Wondai we drive into the quaint ground among the eucalypts down by the golf course. This is where Steve played his senior football and he speaks of it fondly. He scored a lot of tries here. He was in their Under 19s premiership side of 1986. Just a boy, a skinny kid, who the other teams had trouble getting a hand on.

The grounds are well kept, even though there are only junior teams representing Wondai these days. The Wondai Wolves haven't been able to find enough players to field a senior side for some time. There is a little grandstand and a trimmed hedge and gates that tell you whose patch you're entering.

We drive on. I ask Steve whether he knows much of the Indigenous history of the area and whether he knows much about his people. Who are his people? Where is their country? It's something he hasn't spent much time thinking about. He's very open about it. He conveys a sense of regret that he knows so little about his heritage, and it is something he hopes to explore. He reckons it's time to start looking. He feels it.

The country turns to scrub. Over Barambah Creek. To the town in which Steve grew up: Murgon. Population: 5000. Steve points out the golf club, then the meatworks, and Zelinski's Engineering. The shrubs and trees in the middle of the divided road suggest civic pride. We drive up into town, past the South Burnett Aboriginal Housing Co-op, past the real estate agents and the clothing shops and the cafes. Some Aboriginal people sit in the park. They are probably in from Cherbourg, the Aboriginal community ten minutes out of town.

We park and the kids are glad to get out of the car. They race into the sports shop to see their grandad – Elissa's father, Bruce Bishop. He meets them warmly – like a grandad. Then the kids check out the stuff in his shop. Bruce shakes Steve's hand: 'G'day, Bucko.' They seem to be good friends.

Bruce has been a farmer for much of his life. He has tried to retire but things keep popping up, and at the moment he owns a Strudwick Sports Stores franchise. The Reebok rep is in town for the first time in years. She is stoked to be chatting with Steve Renouf. She has that I'm-talking-to-someone-famous demeanour. Steve is as unaffected as always and does everything to deflect the acclaim. She asks for his autograph.

The kids are bundled back into the car and we drive up past the art deco town hall, past Tiernan's pub, and around the corner. There are more Aboriginal people sitting under the trees in the park. The divided road continues out of town to Cherbourg, formerly known as the Barambah Mission. But we don't go that way. We turn into Palmer Street and come to No. 31: the Renoufs' house. Steve's family have never lived in Cherbourg. They have always lived in town. As Aborigines, this placed them in an unusual social position; it was something that had a significant influence on how Steve saw the world.

No. 31 is an old weatherboard house on the corner. There are toys and plastic containers and other bits and pieces strewn around the yard. A small bike leans up against the wall. This is where Steve spent much of his later childhood and youth, before he left for Brisbane. The original verandah has been closed in with those aluminium-framed windows that you see advertised on country television stations. Steve's mother comes to the door. 'Ay, Bucko,' she says.

There is no exaggerated greeting but she is obviously thrilled to see her son and the grandkids. Steve introduces her to me: 'This is my mum, Nerida Renouf'. We are invited into the verandah-room. Mrs Renouf shoos away a couple of her other grandkids – Dwayne and Michael-Paul, teenage boys in American basketball gear who are hanging out at Palmer Street – off the kitchen chairs. The boys don't protest. We sit down. There is a box of kittens and a mother cat which doesn't look old enough to have had them. There is an open Bible on a small table. Steve tells me that in summertime, before the verandah was closed in, they'd bring the mattresses out there to sleep on in the still, hot nights.

Nerida Renouf is a little shy. She is a woman in her late sixties. She has straight hair and her face is initially expressionless. We

have a cup of tea. Steve asks about what's been happening. Every
time a name is mentioned Mrs Renouf explains the family's
relationship with that person. It is important to her to identify
the connections.

Gradually she starts to tell a few stories. She laughs and her
face comes to life. She tells me about her children – all twelve of
them. Steve is the tenth. She says they were all ratbags. And she
thinks I want some dirt on Steve. 'Ol' Bucko: he was always a pretty
good kid,' she says with a grin, '"Cept for the matches when he
nearly burnt the house down! The cupboard's on fire and Bucko,
he took off.' She laughs. 'I found him in bed – under the covers.'
She laughs again. But her taunting is playful and she is clearly
proud of all of her children.

Mrs Renouf takes us through the house. Somehow it has
survived the activity over the years. The walls are scuffed and
damaged in places. The grandkids have used the couch as a tram-
poline. There is stuff everywhere: clothes and boxes of papers and
clutter. There is a cabinet with a broken door which is chock-a-
block with trophies.

It is not a household where material concerns are given
priority. What matters are the people who have called this place
home. Their stories are told on the walls. There are photos of the
children and the grandchildren: a portrait of the beautiful Sonia
('You're a good-looking bunch, you Renoufs,' I say); a photo of Steve
looking angelic at 12 with his sisters and nephews and nieces;
a framed Australian jumper from the 1994 Kangaroo Tour; a
photo of Steve playing for the Murgon Mustangs Under 17s;
Steve's wedding photo; a black and white photo of Charlie's dad
(Steve's grandfather) taken with his dog at Apple Tree Creek near
Childers in the Isis district; a photo of Frankie Malone, the
brilliant Aboriginal footballer who was for a time partner of
Steve's sister Debbie; an original Aboriginal painting; a couple

of shadow boxes. There is a portrait of Mrs Renouf's mother, Eileen South, painted by Charlie Chambers. She looks like a real character – and she was. Hers is a remarkable story.

We walk through the bedroom and the sleepout where somehow the kids all fitted in. 'Three in a bed,' Steve says, laughing. He points out where his posters of Hugh McGahan and Terry Fahey were. It seems amazing that such a big family could have lived together in this modest place.

The back yard is small. There's a basketball hoop and an old corrugated-iron tank. There is a Chinese elm which provided the shade for Christmas dinner every year. We return to the verandah and Mrs Renouf starts to tell me the story of her mother and of her own early life.

We are interrupted when Paul Bishop arrives to pick up the kids and take them out to the farm on the Gayndah Road. There is a double link to Paul. He is Elissa's cousin and he is married to Steve's sister Colleen. The two couples are very close, brought together by their blood relationships, their love of sport, and the fact that both couples had to fight against community prejudices for their relationships to survive.

The kids jump into Uncle Paul's car and there is general cheering that the wait to see their cousins is over.

Mrs Renouf returns to the story of her mother. She tells of being moved around during the 1930s and of coming to Barambah. Steve listens intently. I get the impression he's never heard the whole story. I am inquisitive but we are short on time and there will be another day to sit with Mrs Renouf. Perhaps Steve could be there that day as well.

Steve and I are keen to see the town he grew up in. From 31 Palmer Street you can see the Murgon football ground. It is just 200 metres up the slope to the back gates, but we drive around to the front. There is a big old wooden grandstand. We sit in it together eating some lunch: hamburgers from the service station. You can imagine the stand filled with rosy-faced farmers and their well-dressed wives, townsfolk screaming for the Murgon Mustangs, players' girlfriends with '80s hair and wearing too much make-up. You can imagine matches played with feeling – Cherbourg against Murgon – the tension in the crowd and the nervous faces of the officers of the Queensland Police Force.

This is where Steve played his junior footy. We walk out onto the field. A sprinkler flicks away in the corner. We stand together on the turf wicket in the centre and Steve's face is filled with memories. 'I love this place,' he confides. 'I can be myself in Murgon. I don't have to worry about anything. I love it here.' This is Steve's country.

You can get on to Palmer Street through the back gates of the football ground. Before the Renoufs moved to No. 31 they lived in a run-down old Queenslander on the top corner. The house has been knocked down but the trees in the big yard form a dot-to-dot of where the house used to be. It was the last house on that edge of the town. We drive past it, and head around the corner and down the road until we come to a dirt track. (I knew there was a reason for the four-wheel drive.) 'I'll take you down to Spider's,' Steve says. 'Spider's Bridge.'

We stop at a makeshift gate. Steve is surprised; maybe a little disappointed. 'It must be private property now,' he concludes. It's like the returning-home scene in a movie. We go through the gate. There are a few cow pats around. Steve looks concerned.

Huge gum trees reach skywards. We come upon a stretch of still water: a serene billabong with birds and reeds and Australian blop-blop billabong noises. Crows fark. The creek flows gently from one end. The massive weathered grey trunk of a fallen eucalypt lies on the creek bank and juts into the water so you can walk out along it. The white ants have not touched it. It's been there for as long as Steve can remember, lying like a fallen column in the ruins of a building of ancient Greece. At Olympia or somewhere.

We walk along the creek in the shade, disturbing frilly-neck lizards which launch themselves from overhanging branches into the water and then swim madly, heads up like Kerrod Walters. There are dragonflies in the afternoon sunshine. They zip around touching the water and making delicate ripples on the surface.

We stand and watch. Steve is quiet for a few moments. Then he says, 'This is a great place. Used to come here all the time. Swim. Fish. With Dad. He loved it here.' Charlie died a decade ago.

We walk further and come to Spider's Bridge. It is a dilapidated wooden structure, yet it gives its name to the whole area. I wonder what the local Aborigines call this beautiful place. Steve doesn't know the Aboriginal name. For him it is just 'Spider's': a place to come every day after school with his mates and his brothers and sisters and muck around and walk home in the evening thunderstorms. His place. Significant for his reasons. And still significant.

We head back into town. Past 'The Star', for many years a grand picture theatre and now an antique shop. Past Steve's primary school with its old wooden classrooms and verandahs, geraniums and pepperina trees, and little footy posts. Past the Murgon Jubilee Swimming Pool, full of youngsters on holidays. Past the high school with its baby grandstand and footy oval where every morning there would be a big game of touch, made up mainly of kids from Cherbourg.

We head out along the Gayndah road to visit Paul and Colleen. At the farm the cousins are all playing together and having a ball. Swimming. Riding the Honda 75. Helping Uncle Paul load the pigs. Eating chips. Elissa's mother, Jenny, arrives to see the grandkids, and we sit and chat. You can tell she's Lis's mum. And then it's time to make the three-hour trip back to Brisbane.

The kids fight a bit and then they get sleepy. Steve talks about his early days at the Broncos. About how much he hated the training. About how he was often at the back of the pack, with Wally and Greg Dowling. And about how much he loved playing – and scoring tries. It wasn't even about winning. Just playing. We talk about Wayne Bennett who has been a friend and mentor.

With the petrol gauge precariously below empty (Lis will attest to Steve's notorious absent-mindedness), we are at the Renouf homestead again. Lis comes down. Yep, it was a terrific day.

I get in the Beetle and head back towards Brisbane. I think about the day. And about Steve. He has been one of the great footballers. Blessed with this talent of speed and grace of move-ment. Able to read the play. He's won games for the Broncos and for Australia. And for English club side Wigan.

But the more I get to know him the more I realise that footy is only part of his life. It has allowed him to express his talent. It has taken him places. It has brought enduring friendships. It has set him up for life financially. It's been a huge influence and Steve wants to acknowledge the significance of rugby league in his life. But for Steve football is not everything.

Some of us start thinking about who we are at a young age. We look at our family background, where we are from and what has happened to us. We have stories – myths – which help us to develop a sense of ourselves. We are constantly readjusting our understandings. Perhaps brilliant sportspeople are distracted from this kind of search by the demands of their craft, and by the culture of their sport.

I wait for the red lights to stop flashing on the railway crossing at Ferny Grove. I sit there wondering whether Steve has approached me to write this book because he wants to find out a little more about himself. Perhaps his heart is pushing him to understand his past. Perhaps he wants to know why he was able to stick with professional footy when other Aboriginal recruits from Murgon and Cherbourg found the circumstances too alien. Perhaps he wants, in his own small way, to help Aboriginal people believe that they can do what they hope to do. Perhaps he wants to acknowledge the role of Lis, a woman of tremendous character and determination, and the significance of his family.

I drive past Lang Park again. He could certainly play football. And home. My wife, Susan, asks me, 'How was it?'

I say, 'There's a lot to Steve Renouf.'

CHAPTER 1

Family Heritage

YOU'RE AT HOME watching the tele. A team of fit, strong young men run onto the football field. They appear through the haze of smoke, through the rain of fireworks shrapnel. They're in the Broncos' strip, or the maroon of Queensland, or the green and gold of Australia. You're a bit excited, a bit pumped up. You wouldn't want to be anywhere else – except at the game itself. The last of the fireworks are going off in the background as the familiar voice of Ray Warren fills your lounge room.

You've probably had a few beers and half (nearly three-quarters actually) a Pizza Hut Supreme (no anchovies) and you're looking forward to the sporting spectacle which is about to unfold. You have every right to be expectant because you've seen plenty of great footy matches over the years and the two teams are going to be fair dinkum tonight. You're thinking about how the game will unfold.

Your team is made up of *your* boys. You love them. You feel you know them. You really do. You know something of them from the way they play. They have on-field personalities. They have on-field character. You also know something of them as young men. You have seen profiles of them in the *Courier-Mail* and the *Sydney Morning Herald* and *Rugby League Week*. You have seen them on *The Footy Show* and heard them on *Sports Today* and the ABC's *Grandstand*. You probably know a little of where they are from, and how they got to be playing among the world's best rugby league footballers.

But most of us know only a little about them, in the same way that we don't know too many details about our own family history, our own identity – until we go looking. So we don't know where they have come from, and what has made them. We don't have much of an idea about who they *really* are.

Throughout his career, when Steve Renouf ran onto a footy field we knew he was an Aboriginal bloke from Murgon. We knew he had a rare brilliance that a lot of Aboriginal players seem to have. But we didn't know his story. Not just the story of how he came to top-level football, but his family story; the story that makes Steve Renouf who he really is.

At the Renouf family home in Palmer Street, Murgon there is a painting of Steve's maternal grandmother, Eileen South. The artist, Charlie Chambers, has portrayed her as an old woman, in her eighties perhaps. She holds a walking stick with a carved snake's head on the top. Her face is weathered, yet it has a liveliness. She looks at you: a dignified woman with a thousand stories. Despite all the injustices she battled, despite the impediments placed before her by the attitudes of her times and the laws of the day, her face expresses triumph. She passed on, as the Renoufs say, in 1990. But she lives on in the painting, and in the legacy of her rich life. She had an impact on many people.

Eileen South was born around 1900. Her father, Jim Crollick, was an Englishman. Her mother was Minnie South, sometimes known as Minnie Roberts, an Aboriginal woman of the Gungari people of south-western Queensland.

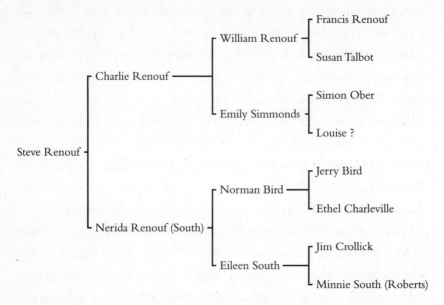

Steve Renouf's family tree

As a young child Eileen was taken from Minnie by the authorities, along with her sister Dora and her brother Alfred. Steve's mother, Nerida, tells the story:

> Mum always told me that she was going to the Mungallala School [west of Mitchell] with her sister Auntie Dora and her brother, Alfred. But the police took them and locked them up in a shed and had them there for three days. I'm not sure whether they fed them or not. They didn't have toilets, and they didn't have a bath for the time they were there. Then Mum and Auntie Dora was taken to Deebing Creek and then put into Purga Mission outside of Ipswich, and that's where she grew up.

For many years Steve's grandmother went by the name of Eileen Crawley. She went to work at Rockybar Station near

Chinchilla. She had a daughter named Iris and then she moved to Cherbourg. At Cherbourg she was thrilled to find her mother, who was known in the settlement as Minnie South. So Eileen Crawley took on the family name and became Eileen South.

At that time Cherbourg was called the Barambah Aboriginal Settlement. In 1897 the Queensland Parliament had passed the Aboriginals Protection and Restriction of the Sale of Opium Act. This placed Aboriginal people under the authority of a Protector whose department had total control over the lives of anyone they deemed to be Aboriginal. The department controlled where Aboriginal people lived. It controlled where and how they worked. It controlled their movement. Aboriginal people had to seek permission to travel. It even controlled the money of individual Aboriginal people.

This was a severe system of oppression which disregarded the hopes and aspirations of Aboriginal people, and cut them adrift from their traditional ways. They were rounded up and forced onto missions, where they were often treated poorly and sometimes inhumanly. Their individual and collective identities were eroded.

Barambah was considered to be a 'dumping ground'. It was not made up of a single mob; it was a collection of disparate people from numerous mobs around Queensland, which further complicated things.

Historian Ken Edwards argues that sport provided one of the few positive experiences for inmates (as they were called) at Barambah at that time. These were the days of Eddie Gilbert, the Aboriginal fast bowler who played cricket for Queensland and could well have played for Australia had he not faced such prejudicial views.

Cricket was popular at Barambah during the 1930s, but rugby league was even more popular – and significant. The teams that wore the green and gold of Barambah helped build the spirit of the Aboriginal community.

Perhaps the greatest player in the crack Barambah football sides of that era was Frankie Fisher, an athletic, powerful and creative centre or five-eighth. He also coached the side. His immense talent has been carried into the later generations of his family. Cathy Freeman is Frankie Fisher's granddaughter. Coming into Cherbourg today you cross the Frankie 'Bigshot' Fisher Bridge over Barambah Creek.

One of the Barambah boys in those sides of the 1930s was Norman Bird. A fine footballer, he was the son of an Aboriginal tracker, Jerry Bird. His mother was Ethel, an Aboriginal woman, sometimes known as Ethel Charleville.

Norman Bird had a relationship with Eileen South which produced two children, Nerida in 1935 and Selwyn in 1937. When pregnant with her fourth child, Jim, she left Norman and Barambah and returned to the Purga Mission where she had spent time as a child and where a number of her people lived. But she moved on from there as well. Nerida takes up the story:

> Mum left Selwyn and Iris [her first child] with Auntie Laura and she run away to New South Wales. I was only two and a half years old when she ran away. My father [Norman Bird] wanted me and she didn't want to give me up so she took me with her. We were in New South Wales until 1945 at Mooli Mooli just outside of Woodenbong just over the [Queensland] border. We lived in the mission and Mum used to do day jobs for Constable Stock and also for Charlie Mason who had the bus run. She used to do housekeeping.

Nerida was very happy growing up in Woodenbong with her mother and younger brother, Jim. 'It was wonderful,' she remembers.

They were beautiful days: swimming, fishing; we learnt to ride horses. Someone gave Jim a rabbit trap – Mum used to cook the rabbits up for us. There was no restriction put on us. We could walk into town . . . We had a lovely teacher, Mr McBride. He was the most wonderful man. Me I'd be yap, yap, yap, yap and he'd say, 'Nerida, shut up talking.' But they weren't strict like they were out here at Cherbourg. Mum should have stopped in New South Wales. It was a good community. It was a happy community. They used to have their babies at home. The Aboriginal ladies would deliver the babies. Everybody helped.

During that time the seeds of Nerida's strong Christian faith were sown. As a child she became part of the Salvation Army. She remembers that when she was about five she said to the Salvation Army officer, Mr Soper, 'I want to give my heart to the Lord.' And he said, 'Nerida, I think you've already done that!' She has gone to church ever since.

But the family suddenly returned to Cherbourg in 1945. Nerida explains:

We left for Cherbourg because, we only found out later, Mum was pregnant to old Charlie Mason [with Hazel]. Coming back, it wasn't very nice. Every afternoon after school kids would be fighting. The language they used to use was something terrible. When I came to Cherbourg, they said, 'At least Nerida has manners'. Even though there was a creek we weren't allowed to swim in it. I lost interest when I came to Cherbourg . . .

I was in Cherbourg until 1954 when we came to live in Murgon. Mum went to Brisbane to work for Mr Semple at Indooroopilly for a while. She left me in the dormitory at Cherbourg . . . My father Norman Bird, he still lived at Cherbourg. He was an overseer and policeman at Cherbourg and he was a forestry worker.

I didn't have a lot of contact with him other than through his roles at Cherbourg. But that didn't worry me. I was a happy-go-lucky kid. I just wanted to enjoy myself with the other kids. I just wasn't interested in all that stuff that was going on around me.

When Eileen South came back from Brisbane she sought to be 'exempted'. At that time individual Aborigines could apply for exemption from the Act, which altered their legal position in the state of Queensland. If granted, they had considerably greater freedom.

Eileen was granted exemption. She took her children and everything she had and left Cherbourg for Murgon. It was a decision of courage, forthrightness and independence. It was also risky: she would have to find somewhere for her family to live, and some way of keeping them. She needed a house and a job, in a community where the racist attitudes of colonial times were deeply entrenched, and Aborigines were looked upon with deep suspicion. Aborigines were not included in the national census until some years later.

Nerida remembers making that trip into Murgon:

The taxi driver tried to get us a house in town but the council and the people wouldn't agree with it so we stopped out along the road. No one would give us a home. The people of Murgon wouldn't give us a home. Only one old white fella gave us a home. Way out [of town]. We stopped at that place for a while. Mum [got work] doing different odd jobs around the place, like at the police station, until she got a job at Tiernan's [pub]. They had an old shop out the back and Mum lived in that for a while. Then she bought that old shop and had it put out along the road. She'd go there on weekends.'

During the mid-1950s Nerida, now a young woman, worked in various jobs in and around Murgon. They were very tough times. Occasionally she would travel to Brisbane where she would stay for a while.

It was during one of these visits that she met Charlie Renouf.

Hanging in the lounge room at Palmer Street is a framed photo of Steve's paternal grandfather, William John Renouf. He was born in Townsville in 1894, shortly after his parents had arrived in the Queensland colony. His father, Francis James Renouf, had French forebears. Born in 1866 in the Channel Islands, Francis had met Susan Talbot, with whom he had two sons out of wedlock. The couple married in Somerset in 1893, and emigrated to Australia. Susan died in 1900. Francis died in 1946 and is buried at the cemetery in Charters Towers.

William Renouf spent his early years in the north. He enlisted in the 31st Battalion at Enoggera in March 1916 and was sent to train at Broadmeadows just north of Melbourne. The battalion sailed in November, joining the Fifth Australian Division in Egypt before being deployed to the western front. On just their third day in action they fought in the infamous Battle of Fromelles. Over half of the 31st Battalion were killed – 572 men – and many of the others were wounded and gassed in a failed assault that lasted only ten hours. In all, 5533 Australians were lost that night. William was spared, but the battered 31st was rendered incapable and was out of action for many months. They were then involved in numerous campaigns at the Somme, Ypres, Menin Road and the Hindenburg line. William was gassed in one of the battles. These injuries, and the trauma and deep grief of his war experience, were to trouble him for the rest of his life.

When he returned to Australia he settled in the Isis district, cutting cane around Childers. It was tough, physical work and there was the constant danger of deadly snake-bite and Weil's disease, a nasty infection spread by rats. A lot of the cane-cutters stayed in the barracks and camps established for itinerant workers, many of whom were Kanaks, Aboriginals and Chinese.

William Renouf met Emily Simmonds, a black woman who lived in the Childers area. She had been born in Bundaberg. Her father was Simon Ober, who was brought to Australia to cut cane, for very low, if any, wages. Simon took the surname Ober, the name of the tiny Pacific Island from which he came. Emily's mother, Louise, was a full-blood Aboriginal woman with links to the Kabi Kabi people of Fraser Island, and also to Aboriginal people from western Queensland.

William and Emily developed a relationship which produced five children. Steve's father, Charles Edgar Renouf, was one of them. Charles was born in 1928 at Apple Tree Creek just outside Childers. The family had a simple house. During the Depression they had barely enough to eat.

Charlie and his sister Dulcie were very spirited, and throughout their lives they never lost the sense of mischief and humour that had sustained them during that terrible period. Sometimes it got them into trouble. Charlie's first cousin, Cliff Douglas (whose mother, Annie, was Emily Simmonds' sister), grew up with him. Cliff remembers: 'We had nothing. We had no money. But we were happy. We didn't think about it. We went fishin'. Huntin'. We'd try to pinch a few oranges or a watermelon. We'd have to watch out for the blokes firing the scatter guns. We were very happy.'

William Renouf had his own demons – the legacy of his war experience – and could be a stern man. He did his best to provide materially for his family. But some of his ideas had far-reaching, long-term effects on how the children thought of themselves. William insisted that there was to be 'no black talk' in the Renouf home. Consequently, much of the cultural heritage of

Emily Simmonds' side of the family remained buried: the traditional names were never used, the traditional language was not used, the family stories were not told openly.

The broader Renouf family believe there were two reasons for this. One was practical: William did not want his family to identify themselves as Aboriginal for fear that the authorities would intervene – as they had a history of doing. The second was spiritual and emotional: there was a lot of pain associated with thinking of yourself as an Aboriginal person at that time, and William and Emily may have been protecting their children from that. Whatever the reason, it was a position taken by a lot of Aboriginal people in those days.

Yet the flame of Aboriginality was never extinguished in the five siblings. Throughout her life, Dulcie, who did not look obviously black, retained a deep sense of her Aboriginality. She often wrote letters to the editors of newspapers. She always began, 'I am a proud black Australian woman', and she was not one to shy away from defending her rights nor her sense of right. Dulcie was an enthusiastic keeper of family stories, and she was able to pass on a keen sense of identity to her own children. Another brother, Uncle Chillie, passed on a strong sense of Aboriginality to his children as well. And Charlie himself was to become an advocate for Aboriginal justice.

In his late teens Charlie left Apple Tree Creek and went to Brisbane. He worked at various jobs, including time as a night worker at the *Courier-Mail*. He was an athlete and a boxer. Cliff Douglas, who used to help train him, reckons he was very quick and could have made it on the pro-running circuit had he not been so easily distracted – by women. Eventually Cliff got jack of it and he said to Charlie, 'Bugger yuh. If you're not going to be fair dinkum, I'm not going to waste my time looking after you, rubbing you down and stuff.'

The history of Charlie's relationships with women is not easily uncovered. One older man who was close to Charlie says, 'You would use all of your fingers and toes and a few more counting the children he is father to.' Another woman said Charlie had fathered twenty-nine children, and then later remembered two more, to make thirty-one. The acknowledged consensus is twenty-six.

Certainly, he was very popular; a man of character and energy; a man of charisma. Nerida remembers the first time she saw Charlie. It was in Brisbane in 1953. 'Charlie was with another woman,' she recalls, 'and we were sitting there at Roma Street on the grass. She was between Charlie and I but he kept grabbing me on the back all the time. And there were some other girls coming along so I just took off and went to the dance with them. But we sort of got together and when I left down there I had [a son] Bill. But Charlie wasn't interested.'

They had a second child, Eileen, but Nerida lived in Murgon, away from Charlie. She worked at odd jobs. There was often no money and little help from a community which virtually shunned them. At one point she had work cooking meals for Stafford Hermann and her brother Selwyn who were working as farm labourers. She lived in a tent on the property with her two young children. One day the men were burning off the grass. 'I had to take them a feed,' Nerida remembers. 'When I came back the tent was burnt down. I had Billy and Eileen. We had no clothes. Nothing. And did any people from Murgon help me? No way in the wide world.'

Then Charlie came back from Brisbane and he and Nerida went to live in Maryborough. During their two years there they were married and young Charlie was born. Two young cousins, the sons of Nerida's cousin Colin Button, also lived with them.

When they returned to Murgon they were still unable to rent a house in town. So they stayed in Jim Kelly's old place before moving down the railway line to a little house. Three more children (Nerida jnr, Warren, and Hazel jnr) were born. Nerida would always go to Wondai Hospital to have the babies.

As time passed, the community became a little more accepting. 'Once Mum [Eileen South] got that job at Tiernan's as a cook they sort of recognised us then,' Nerida says. 'Then a white fella said we could have a house in town. Then we moved into town down the bottom side of the railway line there. I had Christine and Colleen and then we moved to the big place on the corner [of Perkins Street].'

Charlie, Nerida and their nine kids were very poor. Despite the financial struggle it was a lively household. And there were more children to come.

CHAPTER 2

Childhood

IN 1970 MURGON was a typical Queensland country town, a sleepy place where life didn't appear to be very complicated and not much happened. A few people would wander along the main street doing their shopping. A truck would chug along. Farmers in pork-pie hats would stop for a yarn in the barber shop. But all was not as it seemed. Despite Murgon's ambient pleasantness, and the shire motto 'In Unitate Florescimus' (in unity we prosper), racial tension was ever-present.

The Renoufs were rather visible in Murgon – they were one of the first Aboriginal families to live in the town itself. It was impossible not to notice them, and it was taking a long time for them to be generally accepted.

Some locals couldn't abide them: what was an Aboriginal family doing living in town? Why weren't they out at Cherbourg with the other 'blacks', as Murgon people called them? Others were concerned in their own paternal way: what chance did these poor kids have, so many of them, and Charlie on a labourer's wage? Others thought of them as people like themselves, real people with real lives, just trying to do the best they could.

Some mornings Nerida Renouf, pregnant again, would walk up the main street with her trail of half a dozen kids behind her. Eileen, by then at school, would say hello to each of the shop-keepers. Mrs Holland would greet Mrs Renouf outside the newsagency. 'You know we have Sunday School,' she said one time. Mrs Renouf replied, 'I know.'

In Murgon white attitudes to Aboriginal people were derived from colonial doctrines of racial superiority. Such understandings had underpinned everyday life in the small town for a hundred years, as they did throughout Australia. The ideology was so deeply entrenched that it appeared to be the natural way. Most whites viewed themselves as custodians of advanced civilisation, and regarded Aboriginal people as backward and unable to look after themselves. Power lay with the whites, and Aborig-inal resistance to this view was seen as the cause of racial tension. Violence was never far from the surface. The situation was made more complex by the cycle of lost identity and hopelessness that many Aboriginal people suffered. Most whites and blacks fell into their places in the social relations of the district.

Steven Colin Renouf was born into this community on 8 June 1970. It was an easy birth for his mother at the Wondai Hospital where Dr Lipp assisted. The good doctor had come to know the Renouf family pretty well, having delivered most of Nerida's babies over the years. Steve was her tenth child.

On the night Steve was born Old Charlie and his good friend Steve Button bought a carton of Fourex stubbies from the pub and took the old green Mark II Zephyr for a spin out along the dump road. They lit a campfire and sat around having a few beers and a yarn. Old Charlie wanted to celebrate. And he especially wanted to celebrate with Steve Button. 'We're naming the young fella after you, Bucko,' he said to his mate. Steve Button was known to everyone as Bucko after his father who had been a rough-rider in the bush.

Steve was delighted. He was very close to the Renoufs. His father, Colin Button, was Nerida's cousin – a Gungari man. Colin spent much of his working life in western Queensland where it would have been difficult for him to look after a young boy. So Steve was raised by Nan South (Eileen), or, as he calls her, Mum South. Steve speaks of Nan South with the greatest affection – as family. And the Renoufs think of Steve Button as family: the older siblings think of him as a brother, and the younger siblings as an uncle.

As a child Steve Button lived a simple life in Murgon, making his own fun. He loved sport. He was a footballer and a boxer who fought more than 300 amateur fights before being picked up by the promoter Reg Layton. He had twenty pro-fights in the junior lightweight division and once fought the main event at Festival Hall in Brisbane against Greg Liesegang.

Steven Colin Renouf was named after both Steven Button and Colin Button. Steve Button was called Bucko, Colin Button was called Bucko, and so, from the time he was a toddler Steven Colin Renouf became Bucko as well. The name stuck. It had significance and grounding and hence real meaning. And Steve Button was to have quite an influence on the child named after him.

Steve Renouf was his mother's darling boy: the youngest son surrounded by sisters. Their mother's fondness for him did not go unnoticed by the girls. But he was much-loved by them as well. Billy was the oldest in the family and then came Eileen (Bubby), Charlie (Young Charlie), Debbie, Nerida (Fatso), Warren, Hazel, Christine, Colleen, Steve (Bucko), and later Sonia and Angela.

The first house Steve remembers living in was a place on Perkins

Street not far from the Murgon Showgrounds where the rugby league was played. It was a six-bedroom Queenslander on high stumps, with a big yard. Steve would wake up on winter mornings and wander out to the kitchen where his dad would be sitting in front of the wood stove, a smoke in his mouth, cooking toast on a big fork.

Charlie worked for the local council. His wage was not huge and there was a houseful of kids to look after. They were times of financial struggle. The Renoufs enjoyed few luxuries, but they got by. Sometimes dinner was bread and butter and a cup of tea. The kids shared everything. They had to.

When Steve was very young, the family had to move out of Perkins Street. They were unable to find another place and were left trying to make do at Nan South's near the meatworks on Gesseler's Road. The sisters lived inside 'the hut', while the brothers slept in a tent outside. Nan had a room and a bed of her own. There was no electricity. They cooked with coal irons. And you had to make your way down the yard to a thunderbox. This was, remarkably, the mid-1970s.

After a few weeks at Nan's they moved into 31 Palmer Street, the small house which became home to Steve and his brothers and sisters and also, at times, to some of his nephews and nieces. It remains the family home today, and continues to be a meeting place for the large Renouf mob.

Although the family did it tough (and sometimes needed the assistance of the Salvation Army), there was never an atmosphere of deprivation. Charlie and Nerida would never let that happen. Material hardship was debilitating, but never defeating.

Charlie was a man of hope. He was determined that he and his big family would enjoy life. But, at the same time, a deep internal sadness at the plight of his people gnawed at his heart.

Steve spent his early years immersed in the warmth, the

humour and the sense of fun of the crowded (and sometimes chaotic) household. The Renoufs were a close family. 'We really grew up *together*,' Steve remembers fondly. 'The older ones were around too in those days. We all got on really well. We all looked out for each other. There were always people around.'

The kids slept three to a bed when they were young – head to toe. They fought over who'd get to sleep in which bed, the prime position being in the bed where you could peep through the door to catch a bit of *No. 96*. There'd be giggles as someone noticed a bit more of Abigail than they were supposed to know about.

These were carefree, happy days for Steve. Summer days of swimming in the creek and laughing, and fishing for perch with handlines and worms dug up from the creek bank and more laughing, days of penny turtling, hot days of cricket and thunder-storms and brown snakes in swollen creeks and flooded bridges and Murgon cut off from the rest of the world. Freezing morn-ings of steam-breath and the yard white with frost. Dad heading off to work, and Mum trying to keep things going at home.

It was a huge job for Nerida. She found sustenance and strength in her Christian faith. A member of the Salvation Army, the church she had grown up with in Woodenbong, she attended the weekly service and read her Bible at home. All of her children went to Sunday School because Nerida wanted them to come to know the Christian message.

Steve didn't mind Sunday School. It was just what you did on Sunday morning if you were a Renouf. Initially, though, primary school scared him. He could be a timid child and he wasn't keen on leaving the security of his mother. On the first day he put on quite a turn which left him sobbing and upset. One of his sisters calmed him down. But it didn't take long for him to realise that there was nothing much to fear.

All the Renouf boys and girls were naturally gifted athletes and seemed to pick up any game effortlessly. They loved playing sport – any sport – and were usually exceptional at it.

Young Charlie and Warren were outstanding junior footballers. Steve was going to be a footballer like his brothers and desperately wanted his own footy for his seventh birthday. Completely oblivious to the family's financial circumstances, Steve had convinced himself that his parents would get him one. 'Come the morning,' he remembers, 'and Mum had jocks for me! I was absolutely shattered!'

On that day an uncle visited and seeing the young fella's disappointment went out and bought him a yellow leather Steeden football, the type where the paint cracked when you kicked it. That footy got a real flogging, in the yard and over at the Murgon Showgrounds. Within a few weeks it had turned into one of those worn, brown footies which are the companions of a boy's childhood in a country town.

Steve was often with his great mate Clinton Weier whom he first met in Grade 1. They are still close today. They were independent kids who knew how to have fun, the common joy of their childhood masking any sense of difference. In fact he and Clint, who was also naturally quite dark, had their classmates convinced they were both from Africa.

Despite growing up in an Aboriginal home, Steve did not have a strong sense of himself as an Aboriginal person. He wasn't very conscious of it, partly, he thinks, because he went to a white school. The Renoufs were one of the first Aboriginal families to attend the Murgon State School. Steve never thought of himself as different. And he was accepted by the Weier family, which affirmed that.

Yet Aboriginality was certainly not out of sight, as Steve recalls:

It came up because [by then] Dad was involved in the Aboriginal legal service. But Mum and Dad kept us pretty sheltered from all of that. I saw Dad organising protests. I remember when Joh Bjelke-Petersen [who was the local member for Barambah] came to town one day and Dad was part of the protest. I might have been eight or nine. They might have even done some of the posters at our place . . . I never really talked to Dad about that side of things. We didn't have much to do with our culture as young kids. I don't know why. I don't think it was a conscious thing. I think it was just the way it happened . . . I heard the stories later in life.

There were plenty of stories to tell. Old Charlie was a man of tremendous human warmth. He had a genuine affection for people – all people. 'Dad was so friendly,' Steve recalls. 'He was a bloke who just loved to talk.' In fact, there was a bit of a family joke that if Dad was missing he was probably down town having a chat to someone.

A steady stream of visitors passed through the Renouf household and Charlie loved to clown around, making them laugh. The kids were sometimes embarrassed by his antics, but grew to understand that that was 'just Dad'.

Old Charlie had a deeply felt sense of injustice. He believed in justice for all and was outraged by the ongoing discrimination against Aboriginal people, especially in Murgon. 'All he wanted to do,' says Nerida, 'was help his people.' During those years he tried very hard to.

Charlie was appalled by the way the Murgon police treated the local Murris. He had observed many brutal arrests. Steve remembers: 'Dad used to keep an eye on things. He knew the nights they [Aboriginal people] were drinking, so he knew there'd be stuff going on. We'd go up and sit with him in the car. We'd watch a scuffle and then we'd watch the police come and we'd be there just so he could keep tabs on things.'

In the mid-1970s Charlie gave evidence at an inquiry into police treatment of Aboriginal people in Murgon, particularly in relation to the use of police batons. He believed that the local Aborigines were being unfairly targeted for arrest. Unwelcome in the local pubs, some would drink in public places and then be arrested for public drunkenness. All of the aspects of this situation saddened Charlie. And so he set about becoming an advocate for Aboriginal people.

The 1960s and early 1970s had seen many victories for human rights around the world. In the United States humanitarian leaders like Martin Luther King had fought to overcome discriminatory attitudes to African-Americans. In Australia civil rights activists fought widely held racist views. The success of the anti-Vietnam War campaign gave encouragement to dissenters, and helped them develop the skills of organised activism needed for the social reform that was necessary if Australians – all Australians – were to live in a more just society. The times, they were a changin'. In Murgon, they were changin' very slowly.

Small sections of the legal profession in Brisbane were equally outraged by the human rights violations throughout Queensland. Their commitment to social justice led them to act with local Murris to form a legal service in Murgon. It was not a government initiative; it was the initiative of a group of young lawyers and Aborigines intent on establishing and protecting the rights of Aboriginal people. Charlie was invited to a meeting in Brisbane with a group of solicitors which led to the formation of the Aboriginal and Torres Strait Islander Legal Service (ATSILS) in Murgon.

Charlie was an important figure in the organisation because, living in Murgon, he was not restricted by the laws which made movement in and out of Cherbourg difficult, or at least controlled by the authorities, who could be more than a little obstructionist when it suited them.

At that time, only three decades ago, the Queensland government owned and still controlled everything at Cherbourg. The Aboriginal people there were like chattels of the state, and poorly treated chattels at that.

Charlie insisted that his family would not have the sense of subservience which he believed existed at Cherbourg. He was his own man, a free man. He thought like a free man, and acted like a free man. He wanted his children to have a sense of their own freedom. This is one of the reasons he wanted them to grow up in town. It may also be the reason he sheltered his younger children, or certainly Steve, from his ongoing work with ATSILS.

Charlie was formally employed by ATSILS at times but often he volunteered his services. He was known as the 'the barefoot lawyer'. Every Monday morning he would make his way down to the courthouse. He would ask each of the arrested Aboriginal people there whether they had been drunk as charged. If they had been, they would plead guilty. If they hadn't, they would be defended by ATSILS. Various solicitors – Paul Richards, Wayne Goss (later Queensland premier), Leo White, Denis Walker and Terry O'Gorman (now a civil liberties activist) – were employed by the legal service and ensured that Aboriginal defendants were given legal representation and a fair hearing.

Matt Foley worked there during the 1970s, and continued to do so after returning to Brisbane to take up a position in the Department of Social Work at the University of Queensland. He knew Charlie well. He describes him as a 'fighter for his people'. He remembers Charlie's courage. These were disheartening times for Aboriginal people. The Bjelke-Petersen government was racist, authoritarian and repressive. Old statutes meant that there was one law for whites and another for blacks. At the time of

Steve's birth, under the Vagrants, Gaming and Other Offences Act it was actually an offence for a white person to wander or lodge in company with a native. And this was only a generation ago.

To do what Charlie did required considerable resolve, especially as he acted (most of the time) in an honorary capacity. There was no political support, no community support, no personal support outside of his own family. 'To be out on the stump at the frontline in 1974,' says Matt Foley, 'was tough. Charlie was looked to by the local Cherbourg and Murgon Aboriginal communities. He was out there on his own without the benefit of any legal training or formal status. He was an advocate for the rights of Aboriginal people who had been picked up by the police at a time when the police weren't exactly throwing rose petals down in front of him saying, "How can we help you?" '

Charlie and Nerida also set up an Aboriginal housing cooperative in Murgon, an organisation which is still going today. The South Burnett Aboriginal and Torres Strait Islander Black Housing Company, as it is called, was able to purchase houses in Murgon which were then rented out to Aboriginal people, some of whom had been shunned by local landlords. There was always a waiting list and Charlie did his best.

At times Charlie's efforts put him in a lonely position. He was regarded by some in the white community as a trouble-maker, a stirrer who should have known his place. And sometimes there were Aboriginal people who felt he had let them down, when he couldn't do for them what he had said he would try to do, especially in his role with ATSILS. Often that was for reasons of law; the court would give rulings that could not be argued against.

This upset Charlie. When he felt overwhelmed he would ring his sympathisers in Brisbane – in particular, Foley – and sound off, releasing the steam of his frustration.

Yet he was resilient. He never chucked it in. He won the respect of people in both the black community and the white community and could count many as his friends. Foley describes him as a true comrade.

For many years the racial divide in Murgon remained obvious. It was symbolised by the segregated toilet blocks on the median strip in the main street. Prejudicial views fed on themselves. The incidents of public drunkenness and associated behaviour, and other social problems within the Aboriginal community, served to affirm the stereotypical views which many of the townsfolk held. It was the visible behaviour of *some* Aborigines which served to determine the attitude of people to *all* Aborigines. Sadly the prejudice dominated: being black was enough to encourage strong suspicion. There was a section of the community who believed that blacks were no-hopers until they proved themselves otherwise. The absence of trust was awful and destructive, the cycle entrenched.

Yet in the face of such attitudes, and the sadness they could bring, these were happy times for the Renoufs. They just got on with life. Old Charlie did not push his activism in their home. Neither did Nerida. Although their efforts were obvious to their children, they did not dwell on racial issues, nor encourage their children to highlight their Aboriginal identity. This is a position taken by a lot of Aboriginal people of Charlie and Nerida's generation: that it is easier to put some of the stories to the side.

That Aboriginal people like Nan South could continue to live happy and meaningful lives in spite of the overt prejudice is evidence of their strength, their courage and their generosity of spirit.

Charlie found comfort in humour. He was a great one to take the mickey out of himself. He spoke with a stutter. As a result, his nickname was Ch-Ch-Ch-Charlie. When an Aboriginal man was in trouble with the law, someone would say, 'Don't worry, Ch-Ch-Ch-Charlie will sort it out.'

One time Charlie had some T-shirts made up for his kids. On the front was his photograph with the words, 'This is my Dad, Ch-Ch-Ch-Charlie'. The kids wore them proudly, and with affection.

Lots of relatives loved Charlie. Aunty Dulcie's daughter Glenda remembers how much fun it was to visit Palmer Street. Dulcie and Charlie would have everyone laughing. Charlie was a great one for getting words confused. When he was disgusted with his sister, he'd say, 'I'm discovered with you, Dulcie.' He was wonderful company.

Charlie loved going bush, especially fishing. A typical Sunday afternoon activity was to pile as many of the family as could fit into the station wagon and head to a favourite waterhole. Or even just down to Spider's Bridge where he and Steve were in their element.

The Renouf children felt under no obligation to seek the approval of the community, black or white. They did what their parents had hoped they would do and just got on with life. They were good-looking and easygoing, which helped make them popular. However, there is no doubt that success at sport helped the Renoufs to win acceptance in Murgon.

It hadn't always been like that. But Young Charlie and Warren were becoming local footy stars and the Renouf sisters were also successfully involved in the town's sports clubs. They were filling the family sideboard with trophies in everything from squash to netball to basketball and even darts.

This was the world Steve wanted to be part of.

CHAPTER 3

Junior Football

STEVE RENOUF LOVED football from the start. There was always football in the Renouf household – and footballers. He was always playing touch or kicking the footy around in the back yard with his brothers. Ten years his senior, Charlie and Warren were showing immense promise in the local competition. They were quick and talented and played with tremendous flair.

And then there was Frankie Malone, Cherbourg's brilliant young five-eighth, who was going out with Steve's sister Debbie, and was to be the father of her children. Frankie was often at Palmer Street.

Steve grew up with these young men. He was the little kid who was always hanging around, listening, being cheeky, watching and admiring them. They were his heroes. He was going to be a footballer, just like them.

In the late 1970s Frankie Malone, then in his early twenties, was playing brilliant rugby league. He had sport in his blood. His father, Jack 'Champ' Malone, was a legend of Cherbourg sport from before the Second World War. Champ played half-back with Frankie Fisher (after whom Frankie Malone is named). But he was an even better cricketer. He played in the same teams as the renowned Aboriginal fast bowler, Eddie Gilbert. Opening the Queensland attack in 1931, Gilbert famously dismissed Don Bradman for a duck. Some argue that he would have played for Australia had he been white. To this day Gilbert remains an important symbol to the Murri community that black is not inferior to white.

Champ Malone was a beautiful batsman. He was keen to play cricket at the highest level. The superintendent at Cherbourg, Boss Semple, was convinced he had the ability. In 1939 Semple wrote to the Chief Protector suggesting that Champ be given a chance to play first class cricket. That was as far as it got. There were some who said the process was stalled because the cricket community could not handle the idea of a black batsman. Batsmen were the princes of cricket. And they believed an Aboriginal man could never be a prince. Although he had his supporters, the outbreak of war intervened and the decline of cricket at Cherbourg meant that Champ Malone never got the opportunity to show what he could do.

Frankie Malone inherited his father's natural talent and in doing so he carried with him a tradition of Aboriginal sport. There were offers from the city rugby league clubs, but Frankie continued to play in the strong South Burnett competition.

At the same time, Young Charlie and Warren Renouf, both younger than Frankie, were emerging as stars of that competition. They were exciting prospects, players who got people talking about football and brought them through the gates. Charlie was playing representative football and looked to have a future in Brisbane, if he chose to build a football career down there. He was genuinely quick, a try-scoring winger. But he didn't play for Murgon. He had been lured to Wondai.

Trevor Daley called the football on the local Kingaroy station, 4SB. He and his team sat at a table alongside the footy field. Occasionally a kick for touch would head in his direction and listeners around the South Burnett would hear the sound of papers rustling and microphones bumping and the footy thumping into the table. Trevor loved Charlie. He thought Charlie had something special and whenever the winger loomed Daley's voice would lift, Charlie would lift, the whole district would lift. He made people in their kitchens and on their tractors believe that when Charlie had the football anything was possible. And it was. With his blistering pace, Charlie could score from anywhere.

Trevor didn't just call him 'Renouf', or 'Charlie Renouf', he called him 'Charles Joseph Renouf'. The funny thing was, he was Charles *Edgar* Renouf, like his dad. But somehow that didn't matter. And the tag stuck.

As Warren entered the senior ranks he too was highly regarded. He signed up with the Murgon Mustangs, which pitched him against his brother. Much was made of the Renouf v. Renouf clash when the Mustangs played Wondai. There was a healthy rivalry between the two young men, on and off the field. They would sit around the kitchen table arguing about who was quicker over 100 metres and threatening to go up to the show-grounds to settle it once and for all. They never did.

Trevor Daley knew how quick they were. He was convinced that Charles Joseph Renouf could make the two of them a pretty penny as a professional runner. He trained him for a couple of years and Charlie won a few local events. Stacks of money went on him the day he won the Murgon Lightning. They still remember the celebrations.

Old Charlie didn't go to the football much. But one afternoon he took Steve in the Holden Special to see Young Charlie play in a rep match for South Burnett at Nambour. As Young Charlie went over for his sixth try, Old Charlie looked down at Steve and said: 'You'll be doing that one day.'

Steve wondered, 'Will I?'

Steve watched and listened to his brothers. They didn't teach him to play, as such. He just learnt rugby league from being around them. Occasionally they would make a comment. Steve remembers playing tackle in the back yard for the first time. When he was about to be hit, he jumped, dangerously, and his brothers said, 'No. No. No. Don't do that. You'll break your neck.' And so the lesson was learnt.

Surprisingly Steve was a little late in coming to junior football. Quite a few of his mates had signed on with the Murgon Mustangs when they were seven years old. But Steve was initially reticent and quite doubtful. Even though he was mad keen on the game, he wasn't comfortable with the idea of playing in front of other people.

He didn't join in until he was nine. A junior sign-on day was one of the rituals of Queensland life and the Murgon Mustangs Muster was a classic example. Steve gathered together the necessary items – his birth certificate and his registration fee – and joined the line along with Clint Weier and a few of his school friends. Registered and ready to play, he was officially a footballer.

At training he made new mates in the kids from St Mary's, who joined with the state-schoolers to play for the town. Ted Walton coached the Under 10s. Their first match was at home against Goomeri. Steve's sister Debbie took Steve along. There were a number of thrills for him that day. The first was that he got to kick off, and it was a mammoth boot, he remembers, of about ten and a half metres. Then, with his first-ever touch in football, he scored a try. He got the ball and headed off in one of those huge Under 10 arcs, heading slightly backwards and across field to run around the pack. Striding out, his skinny legs pumping, he outsprinted everyone to the line. And then he scored a try with his second touch. He felt the thrill of it all, of running freely, of beating opponents, and that was it. Rugby league was his game.

He quickly stood out. His gift came in four parts: he could run, he knew where to run, he could change direction, and he could score tries. He was an absolute natural. And he loved it.

He loved everything about football. He loved his Gold Cup footy boots, his smelly old hand-me-down Steeden shoulder pads, even the foam pads that went in the pockets in the side of his footy shorts. (He didn't wear a mouth guard in the early days.) He loved his Valleys jumper: blue with the VFC on it. He loved his footy posters. But especially, he loved *playing* football. Just being out there and getting the ball.

Junior football was structured so that there was an Under 10, an Under 12, an Under 14 and so on. This meant that kids had a year in which they were the younger ones in the team, followed by a year in which they were the senior members. Already by the Under 12s the big arc strategy wasn't so successful, and the lads were starting to find their positions and understand football a bit better. Steve played inside centre for his two years in the Under 12s. Inside him were the Marsden boys – Mitchell at half-back and Stephen at five-eighth. Their family owned Marsden Motors. They quickly learnt the value in spreading the ball wide.

Clint Weier remembers that Steve didn't much like playing against Cherbourg. Cherbourg players would always get stuck into Steve and he was a little hesitant. 'You fuckin' white eye,' they taunted, accusing Steve and his family of seeing the world through white eyes. They also called him a coconut: dark on the outside but white in the middle. He was always targeted on the field, but they never got him.

Steve wasn't overly worried by it all. Old Charlie hated angry argument and upset, and believed that confrontation was to be avoided, a trait he passed on to his children. He had always told Steve that if something was said, whether on the footy field, down town, at school, anywhere, it was best to reply with 'Righto' and walk away. 'Just ignore them,' he used to say, and then he would explain that they didn't know any better, that that was just what they had been brought up to think and that there were prejudices in the Indigenous community as well. Steve could see that, and he wasn't going to be alienated from the Cherbourg Murris because of it. He assumed this was the way it was, and just accepted the situation.

The taunts were watered down when the Cherbourg kids came into Murgon for their high-schooling. Suddenly they were all playing touch footy together, and getting to know each other.

Steve made the Wide Bay primary school team which competed in the state carnival in Bundaberg, and was then selected to play on the wing in the Queensland Country side. He wanted to tell the selectors that he was a centre, but he didn't think it would do any good. Stereotyping seemed to prevail. In those days Steve would hear it all the time: 'You're black, you're fast, so you'll play on the wing.'

Despite beating City 18-2, very few of the country kids made the Queensland primary school team. Steve missed out and, although disappointed, he was thrilled to have had the opportunity to play. The carnival helped him develop confidence, and he was having fun and making friends from out of town.

There were moments of doubt too. Like many kids from the country Steve sometimes felt overawed, as if the world belonged to someone else; that when they went away on footy trips or to representative athletic meetings all the other kids were big and cool and cocky and had the right gear and walked around as if they were about to be signed by Parramatta. When, not long after the Commonwealth Games, Steve first visited the QE II Stadium with the Wide Bay athletics team for the state championships, he was one of just a handful of kids without running spikes. The red synthetic track burnt his feet.

These incidents kept his focus local. He was becoming increasingly comfortable in his home town, as a teenager and as a sportsman. Steve was a Murgon boy.

A few things, seemingly insignificant, helped him grow in confidence. The local ref, Pat Donohue, would sometimes give Steve a wink after he'd scored a try. That was enough for Steve. He started to realise he was a pretty handy player, by Murgon standards.

Steve's family didn't make a fuss about it though. His mum didn't go to his games on Saturday. She didn't really approve of Steve playing football as she thought he was too small. In a photo of Steve, his sisters and his nieces, taken when he was about twelve, he looks more like a choir boy than a rough-and-tumble footballer. His mother was so concerned that at one point she bought Steve a set of clubs in the hope that he'd take up golf.

Old Charlie liked football but he would never actually go into the ground for Steve's games. He would drive the car up to the showgrounds fence and, when Steve was jogging back to halfway after crossing over for a try, he'd flash the headlights to register his attendance and his delight. Those lights always gave Steve a lift. That was his dad.

Football Saturdays were fun. If the Mustangs played away, it was a bus trip to Blackbutt or Kingaroy or one of the other little towns, which always included a stop at a service station. Invariably some kid would flog a packet of Lifesavers or PK – that was one of the traditions of rugby league. And invariably one of the coaches would stand at the front of the bus yelling to find out who the pilferer was. There was plenty of mucking around – and a game of footy.

If they were at home at the showgrounds Steve would hang around after his match for a while before heading back to Palmer Street which was always filled with the racing chant of Vince Curry or Larry Pratt. The form guide would be laid out on the kitchen table. Steve could hardly wait for six o'clock and *The Big League* with Arthur Denovan or Peter Meares and David Wright on ABC TV.

These were terrific years for Queensland rugby league. A good spread of excellent players had the Brisbane competition thriving. And, of course, State of Origin football was just taking off.

What could have been more exciting for a young boy in the early 1980s than sitting in the warm lounge room in Murgon with as many Renoufs as could be crammed in watching Queensland go into battle? In those early years the northerners worked at righting an injustice: that for many years their home-grown stars were made to pull on the New South Wales jumper to play against their own. They were tired of losing many of their talented players to the Sydney competition. The Maroons were always the underdogs and the Renouf mob had no trouble sledging the arrogant Blues. They watched the grand performances of Arthur Beetson and Wally Lewis, and the local South Burnett boy Chris Close.

And Mal Meninga: this immense man who could turn games with his pace and sheer power. Meninga played for Souths, under Wayne Bennett. He was Steve's favourite.

Steve learnt a lot from the television coverage. When Wally Lewis started throwing long spiral passes, so did the lads in the Murgon Under 12s. When Parramatta used the wall a couple of seasons later, so did Steve's Under 14 team. Steve followed all of the footy. A corner of his bedroom was a shrine to Sydney's Easts and his sisters knew that they touched his posters and photos at their peril.

There was also television coverage of the football from Sydney. It seemed so glamorous, somehow grander than the games in Brisbane. And there was the mid-week competition: the Amco Cup which was later called the KB Cup. And all so far away.

Even Brisbane was a long way away.

Steve loved going to the local senior footy matches. He would get there early on a Sunday morning to line up with some of his Under 12 team-mates hoping he'd get picked out to be ball-boy for the three matches that afternoon: Under 19s, Reserve Grade and A Grade. It was $1 a game and as soon as he was paid he'd buy a Murgon pie and a can of Creaming Soda from Mrs Niebling (Bryan's mother) and Mrs Evans at the canteen.

The Murris really lifted the local competition. They were the energy, the life-force which made the matches so entertaining and exciting. A few Murris played for the town teams but most turned out for Cherbourg. Murris had their own style, and that made for spectacular football. They played fast, open football, with a flamboyant creativity that is hard to describe and hard to explain. Steve says it is as if there is some unspoken connection between the players, a faith they have in each other. It is an innate ability and a preference for *playing* football in the true sense of the word. Playing in the sense of enjoyment, and seeing what they could do with the football. There were always games of touch being played by the Murris at Cherbourg. And it was the preferred training drill at the club. This was the way they had played for a number of generations, since the days of Frankie Fisher.

The matches could also be very physical contests and occasionally wild brawls erupted on and off the field, especially when Murgon and Cherbourg met. Football became more than just a clash of two sporting teams or two geographic locations.

Football became a clash of two cultures, a place where deep-seated animosities were angrily expressed. Players threw punches which carried the weight of history, the latent anger of two communities which in many ways, sadly, remained irreconcilably separate.

Sometimes spectators, a-brim with the bravado of amber fluid, charged on to the field to land a few haymakers, and there were occasions when it looked like things would get out of hand. A number of times it did. In one incident, a nasty brawl erupted among the crowd and five policemen were injured.

Violence, controlled or otherwise, was a part of country football in those days. Footy was played by tough men, and watched by tough men – and by women who loved them for it. Steve looked on from the touch-line, a small boy clinging to a Steeden, and if he was ever going to mix it with the men he was watching it was skill rather than brawn that would be his trump card.

Young Charlie's spectacular performances in local games had brought him to the attention of talent scouts from Brisbane. Initially he went down to play for Samford where he scored dozens of tries. Then Wynnum–Manly, who were becoming a force in the QRL competition, thanks to Wally Lewis, Gene Miles and company, showed interest in him. This would mean Charlie had to move to Brisbane, a huge step for an Aboriginal lad from Murgon. His mum certainly didn't want him to go: she didn't want any of her children to move away. Murgon was their home, their place, the place where they could be together. This was what mattered to her, as it did to many Murris.

Charlie decided to have a go. He went to two Wynnum training sessions before coming back to Murgon. It wasn't for him. The sessions were very demanding. He was lonely and felt lost. So he did the obvious thing and came back to the place where he didn't feel lost – and played football at home.

Steve watched all of this unfold. It didn't worry him. In fact he loved having Charlie and Warren at home and these things helped keep his mind focused on Murgon. He wanted to play well enough to be a local champion.

He didn't set out consciously to satisfy that ambition. He didn't set out to learn football. The skills, he says, were just there. He didn't think about it. He just loved to play.

In his early years at Murgon High School Steve was a bit of a ratbag. He was always looking for a laugh, often at the teacher's expense. In Year 8 he would sometimes find himself sitting outside the principal's office. It was the price he paid for being a smart-arse in class.

Life was fun. There were no limitations on his movements and most of the time his parents wouldn't have had a clue where he was. He was usually mucking around with a few of his mates, enjoying the freedom he had. There were no responsibilities.

He was, by his own admission, getting a bit ahead of himself. Presentation nights at the football club ($1 for a steakburger and a can of Creaming Soda) had always been good for Steve and by Year 9 he was cocky. He thought of himself as the bullet-proof local sports-star. Good-looking, athletic and popular, he strutted his stuff around the schoolyard.

He was certainly noticed by Elissa Bishop, who was in his year at school. One day during Year 9 Animal Husbandry he went up to Elissa, flicked her bra-strap, and said, 'What's this for?' And laughed.

Schoolwork wasn't very important to Steve and he did just enough to get by. Long-serving Murgon teacher Greg Smith taught him Maths in Year 8 and remembers Steve's first year at high school: 'He was a skinny little kid who was a good athlete, but at that time he didn't look like a football player'. Over the years he would find out how off the mark his first impression had been.

Steve was cheeky but always good-natured, never a trouble-maker. He looked forward to playing in the schoolboy sides. And at club level he was making his way through the junior grades for the Mustangs, scoring tries and enjoying his footy. Kev Robinson coached him for his two Under 14 years. Then Steve Button took over.

Button was a good sportsman himself. After marrying, he had moved to Cherbourg where he was invited to coach the football side. He took them to two local premierships. From there he started coaching his son's under-age side at the Mustangs and eventually he was put in charge of Steve's team. He coached them for four years – to four premierships. Steve Button meant a lot to Steve Renouf because he had always been around and he brought together the three central elements of Steve's life: family, Murgon and rugby league.

Button was amazed by Steve's ability. Right from the outset he saw that Steve had pace and balance and an instinct which allowed him to see how football worked. He knew when to run and where to run. He had great timing.

Watching the young star in the Under 14s, two years before he became his coach, Steve Button said to Old Charlie, 'This fella'll play for Australia.'

Charlie was surprised: 'Is he that good?'

'You wait,' Steve Button said confidently.

Steve Renouf never thought he'd go that far. He was just hoping to eventually make it in Murgon. He continued to play inside centre, and continued to score tries. He seemed to hit top pace in a couple of strides and could find a hole in any defence. People were starting to take notice. There were some who wanted him to have a go in senior football, even when he was still physically immature.

His mother would have none of that. Already she was concerned for him. One day Steve received a nasty knock to the head. He went to bed early that evening feeling a bit crook. Not long after, he got out of bed and went for a wander. One of the others yelled out, 'Hey, Mum, Bucko's sleep-walking.' He made it into the front yard where he tackled Old Charlie to the ground, saying, 'Where's my orange? Where's my orange?' He was out of it. They put him back to bed. He went off to the doctor the next day. He was fine. The following week his mother bought him headgear which she insisted he wore whenever he was playing. From then on Steve always wore his distinctive headgear.

The Renouf household seemed more crowded than ever. But it was a happy place. The kids loved their dad – even if he did play Charlie Pride and Jimmy Horton and The Seekers. Mrs Renouf held it all together, working and working to keep them all going. Steve was often frustrated with how hard she had to work, especially in caring for her nephews and nieces. Sometimes she'd get fed up and the whole household knew to clear out and give her some peace – even Old Charlie. So off the kids would go to Spider's.

Steve could be a handful as well. One day, not long after starting high school, he learned where some of his natural pace came from. When he dropped his dirty footy socks on the floor his mother chipped him. He picked them up and threw them at her. She grabbed the smelly socks and took off after him. And, she says proudly, 'I caught him. He couldn't get away from me. He couldn't outrun me!'

The week's routine was bordering on chaotic. Someone always had to go somewhere. Steve's younger sister Sonia was a talented young sportswoman. For a couple of years her week was netball on Monday; senior squash on Tuesday; junior squash, volleyball and sometimes indoor soccer on Wednesday; basketball on Thursday; going out on Friday; netball on Saturday; and on Sunday she'd watch Steve play football. Mrs Renouf knew her kids weren't getting into trouble, because they were always playing sport.

Steve's sporting week was also hectic. He tried most sports, and was pretty good at every one of them, except swimming. 'Blackfellas aren't known for their swimming,' he once told *Today Tonight*.

By comparison with his busy sporting life his school day was pretty cruisy: breakfast at home before heading up the track to Nan South's where he'd have a second breakfast, then to high school to see what was happening, a bit of schoolwork, then off to footy training.

As a youngster, Steve was a notoriously bad trainer. He couldn't see the point. He wanted to *play* football, and if not football, a game of touch was enough. He couldn't see the value of formal, structured training and, according to Steve Button, didn't exert himself. Many times when Button had them doing a drill, Steve would whinge, 'Do we have to do this?'

Even at representative training he didn't put in too much effort. He was a permanent fixture in the Wide Bay team and, in making the Queensland Under 16 side, was the first Murgon Mustangs' junior to be selected for his state. (Bryan Neibling had had to wait until he was playing senior football.) One day Wayne Bennett was invited up to Nanango to take training. Steve met him for the first time. 'He was gruff,' Steve remembers. 'We thought he was a bit grumpy. And he flogged the crap out of us. He probably noticed that I pulled out of that session. I think I had a bit of an injury.'

It was the same with school training. Greg Smith had helped

make Murgon High School a rugby league school. He coached the open team from 1970 to 1997. Despite its comparatively small number of enrolments, Murgon High built a terrific reputation in the celebrated Commonwealth Bank Cup, and the school dominated the local Pioneer Concrete Shield.

Smith saw a remarkable number of gifted players come through the school. Some went on to senior football. Some didn't. Of the Murri boys from around Steve's time, Gordie Langton made the 1985 Australian schoolboys team and later played with Alfie Langer at the Ipswich Jets. Dodo Harrison also made the 1986 Australian schoolboys team but never went on. The Bird boys – Mike, Ricky and Dion – were all talented. (Steve played against Dion many years later in his two seasons in England.) Jack Simpson also went to the Jets. Bevan Costello was outstanding. Stafford Sandow went to Brisbane, played one game of Reserve Grade with the Broncos, and then returned to Cherbourg.

It was tough for the Murri lads when they moved to the city for football. The pull of family loyalties and traditions (Smith calls it 'the Cherbourg magnet') was strong and often they didn't stay away for long. Many didn't play at the level they might have, had their aspirations been different.

Greg Smith had an idea of how good Steve could be, but he also knew it would take discipline to get anywhere – even at schoolboy level. Natural talent could only get you so far in football. Yet during those high school days Smith saw Steve develop without having to work hard at all. He was a terrific player in a reasonable side in Year 11.

That year Murgon High played Maroochydore High in the Pioneer Concrete Shield in an early curtain-raiser to a Test match against New Zealand. It was Steve's first match at Lang Park. He remembers the buzz of running on. 'How thick is this grass?' the boys were saying to each other. 'It was so thick,' Steve remembers, 'you even felt slow. Your feet sank right in.' It was quite different from the tightly cropped South Burnett grounds, worn down by constant traffic and the winter frosts.

By Year 12 Steve was a sensation. Murgon High had a useful pack, but the back-line was full of Murri brilliance. Smith had them work a narrow blind, and then use the expansive open side, to give Steve plenty of room. 'He was a freak,' Smith recalls. 'He had this incredible balance, this incredible ability to stay on his feet, this incredible pace and an incredible ability to score tries. He could just read a game.'

All this may have happened on the field, Greg says, but off the field Steve was lazy. He hated training (sometimes he wouldn't even turn up), and remarkably he wasn't overly fit. He also wasn't a natural leader in a conventional sense. He wasn't a player who'd walk around patting others on the bum and encouraging them. He had other talents. Already he was a performer. He concentrated on his own game, quietly doing what it was he could do. In fact he had asked Greg not to make him captain in that final year, but to give the captaincy to Brett Plowman who had decided to repeat Year 12 (and would go to the Canberra Raiders the following season before eventually playing with Steve at the Broncos).

By this stage Steve had become good friends with the Smiths. Greg's wife, Carmel, the school's deputy principal, had a soft spot for Steve and Clint Weier. They were kids with plenty of life and plenty of character. Greg had Steve in Maths in Society, along with Leah Purcell, a relative of Steve's who these days is a celebrated singer and actor. They would try to get Greg talking about football – and were often successful.

Greg knew Steve desperately wanted to make the Queensland and Australian schoolboy sides in his final high school year, 1987.

In Bundaberg, he was voted player of the state carnival and was picked for Queensland. The *South Burnett Times* ran an article under the headline 'South Burnett breeds new champ' with a photo of a grimacing Steve. The local community was starting to make the young Aboriginal man their own. 'Steve Renouf is the latest discovery in the long line of top-quality players bred in the South Burnett,' the reporter wrote proudly. 'The classy centre attends Murgon High School. His state selection continues a strong tradition in that school, which has seen four other players chosen for the Queensland Schoolboys in the last four years. Two wingers, Gordon Langton and Darryl Harrison, have gone on to play for the Australian Schoolboys.'

Everything seemed to be going well for Steve Renouf. He was very happy. He was fast becoming a local football star.

And he was in love.

CHAPTER 4

Lis

THERE ARE MANY enduring images of rugby league. It is a game of violent confrontations, some within the rules, some not. Some games are fair; some are callous. There are bone-rattling body clashes. Some images stay with us: the bloodied warriors leaving the battlefield, the all-in stoushes, the huge hits. There is a famous photo of a bloodied and exhausted Benny Elias after Origin III in 1992. There is the footage of Mick Devere on the sideline having his head stapled. Television coverage of State of Origin matches is often introduced with a montage of celebrated biff, and we find ourselves full of lounge-room aggro.

Steve Renouf has mixed it with the best of them, in his own way, and has made a name for himself in this rather blokey sport. Yet some of the most influential people in Steve's life have been women – very strong women. His mother, of course, is an ongoing model of resilience for Steve and the extended Renouf family, as was his grandmother, Nan South.

Steve also grew up surrounded by sisters, all of them active, talented and competitive. They grew to be strong women, proudly Renouf, proudly Aboriginal. Steve's older sisters developed a conscious sense of their Aboriginal identity before he did.

The other vitally important woman in Steve's life is his wife, Lis. You cannot make sense of what has happened to Steve Renouf unless you understand Lis and the relationship they enjoy.

Everyone you speak to – Steve's mother, his siblings, the Bishop family, Wayne Bennett, Clint Weier, indeed all those close to Steve – acknowledges that Lis had a vital role in supporting Steve to become a household name in Australian rugby league. Lis is a very determined woman and she was determined that Steve would go as far as he could in football. Steve always had the ability, but without the encouragement and insistence of Lis only the South Burnett would have known his brilliance.

Elissa Bishop had a happy childhood growing up on the farm with her father, Bruce, her mother, Jenny, her older sister, Leah, and her younger sister, Regina – and her animals. She enjoyed a rich country lifestyle.

Bruce's family had settled in the district in the late 1930s. His father, Reg, and mother, Gill, had moved up from Sydney, having purchased 'Hyning', a property outside Murgon. They had five boys and a girl, Bruce being the second youngest. The brothers remain very close. 'Hyning' was a family enterprise which eventually went to Philip. Bruce wanted his own place. He bought 'Windera', a mixed farm which included a dairy and a piggery, and he grew crops. He sold 'Windera' to purchase 'Silverleaf' (when Lis was 11) where he grew wheat and barley, soya beans, corn, sunflower and cotton.

Bruce married Jenny Obel, from Kingaroy, the daughter of a Danish immigrant, Sigfred Obel (now, in his nineties, known as Poppy), who had come to Australia just after the First World War, and Audrey Campbell. Audrey died shortly before Bruce and Jenny were married.

Bruce and Jenny built a typical Australian country home: secure and loving, active and enterprising, and full of fun. Lis always had plenty to do. She went to school at Windera State School where, in her first year, the entire school enrolment was nine. (One year there were fifteen students.) Later, when they moved to 'Silverleaf', she went to the busy Mondure State School where there were forty-five students, and then into Murgon High School for Year 8.

Each week the family went to the little Uniting Church at Merlwood (which had previously been a Methodist church). They were a conservative rural family. They had faith that hard work would bring rewards – emotional, spiritual, financial – and that, as much as life was a struggle, it was a battle which could be won. Achievement was valued and encouraged, in a healthy, balanced way. You could only give your best.

Lis wasn't particularly interested in sport. She played tennis on the old antbed courts, but she had absolutely no interest in rugby league. Her father did though. Bruce enjoyed the football and would sneak away from the girls to watch *The Big League* on TV and would make it to some local games. His nephew Paul had played rugby union at Toowoomba Grammar School and, returning to the family farm, was a handy local rugby league player and cricketer.

Lis had other interests. She took piano lessons and was enthusiastic about her Scottish Highland dancing.

She was never one to shy away from hard work. A bit of a tomboy, she was always out there helping: shifting irrigation pipes or looking after the animals. She was her dad's offsider, which he loved, as much for the company as for the assistance. They talked about everything and could natter away for hours. He was very protective, and as much as the girls grew up with a sense of freedom, they also understood there were limits.

One day they were out ploughing together and chatting away when he looked for an assurance from Lis: 'You wouldn't go out with a blackfella, would you?'

At that time relationships between white girls and Murri boys were frowned upon. (They still draw comment in the district today.) Influenced by stereotypical views, some parents worried their daughters would wind up with Aboriginal boys. They continued to hold the entrenched view that Aboriginal people were unreliable, lazy, erratic, and quick to violence, and they presumed that if their daughter got mixed up with a blackfella she would be very unlikely to enjoy a happy and stable home life.

Despite the local prejudices, couples inevitably got together. In some cases when relationships formed, parents removed their daughters from the Murgon High School and enrolled them in Kingaroy or sent them off to boarding school. Indeed, some children went straight to boarding school as a matter of course so they would not be exposed to the tensions in the community.

Lis didn't think much about the matter. But she loved her parents and didn't want to let them down. Whether it was true or not, she *believed* that if she did get together with an Aboriginal lad she would have some explaining to do. She was probably right.

In those early high school years Lis couldn't help but notice Steve Renouf. 'Steve thought he was pretty cool,' she recalls. 'And he was confident. He thought all the girls loved him.' They were in a few of the same classes and Lis started to realise she was quite keen on him. 'I used to miss him on Thursdays,' she remembers, and then explains, 'Steve always had a sickie on Thursdays.'

Steve showed her little attention at first. He was playing the field, looking to pick up girls at the pictures. The balcony at 'The Star' was his favourite haunt – not that he had much luck.

He loved hanging out at Wruck's hamburger shop, and he loved going down to Spider's. He'd ride down on the pushbike, often with Clint. And he loved AC/DC, Sweet, and Cold Chisel.

Right throughout high school the lads were up for a few beers, at parties and dances or on footy trips, always running the time-honoured Australian gauntlet of teachers and coaches and the local coppers. In fact, Steve reckons he was more of a drinker during his school days than at any other time in his life.

Steve and Lis first got together at the school camp at the start of Year 11. It was all very innocent. Nonetheless Lis felt compelled to tell her parents that Steve Renouf was interested in her. 'I told them because otherwise they would have heard around town,' Lis recalls. 'Gossip goes around town. I knew my parents wouldn't have been happy. I would have been in a lot of trouble.'

As it turned out, they went their separate ways until the middle of that year, just as Lis was making the decision to leave school. Lis had always wanted to be a hairdresser, and when an apprenticeship became available at the Cameo Beauty Salon, Lis got the position. That meant spending the first six months at Kingaroy TAFE College half an hour from Murgon by bus. The family farm was out of town, and getting into Murgon, and then to Kingaroy and back, and then back home, made it a long day. So Lis lived in Murgon with her grandmother, which meant that Steve and Lis could spend a lot of time together. 'Every afternoon Steve would meet me down at the TAFE bus and walk me back up towards my grandmother's,' Lis remembers. 'But we couldn't ever walk together to my grandmother's because if she saw me we'd be in trouble, because he is an Aboriginal. So we used to just stop for a while behind an old truck on a vacant allotment. Then he'd turn around and walk back home and I'd go off to my grandmother's.'

It was a difficult time, but Lis knew how she felt. 'It annoyed me,' she explains, 'but there was no other way. We were just happy to be seeing each other.' Of course, being a small town, people didn't miss anything. 'It did come out,' Lis says. 'One day Mum said that it had got around that we were together, and that's when Mum and Dad tried to stop it.'

The Bishops did have their concerns, and the memory of this time is a delicate issue. It came to a head at a school musical dress rehearsal after Lis had started her apprenticeship. She and Steve were sitting holding hands in the mezzanine level of the Town Hall, alongside a friend, Andrew Shailer, who was controlling the lighting. Unbeknown to the young couple Bruce was walking up the stairs. Andrew could see him coming and, to use Lis's words, 'Andrew knew that it was wrong for Steven and I to be together but he couldn't say anything because my father was coming up. So Dad sprung us together and there was this big thing that I probably shouldn't be with Steve.'

Lis says memories of those early days are difficult for her parents. She remembers their apprehension and initial concern. 'It wasn't that they didn't like Steve,' she explains. 'It was just because he was an Aboriginal bloke. They weren't prejudiced or anything, they just didn't want *their* daughter to be going out with an Aboriginal. But after that, once Dad met Steven, there was maybe a week of "perhaps you shouldn't be doing this" but they then accepted him for who he was. Right from then.'

It helped that Lis was strong-willed. She says, 'I knew that as long as Steve looked after me and treated me right there wasn't that much they could do. And give Dad and Mum credit, they knew what I wanted and they accepted that.'

Steve knew that things might not work out. When a previous relationship had developed with a white girl, she had been shifted away from Murgon to another school. It was just, as he always says, the way it was.

Lis knew that Steve was very keen. And the two of them were willing to fight for their young love, in the face of any community prejudice.

Around that time Colleen Renouf, the sister immediately above Steve, was going out with Paul Bishop, Lis's cousin. This caused some consternation in the Bishop family as well. But the couple grew closer and eventually announced their engagement. On a Mad Monday after footy season, Paul proposed to Colleen on the see-saw in the park. They went straight up to ask Old Charlie at Palmer Street. He was delighted and afterwards always joked that now that Paul Bishop had pinched one of his daughters he'd have to get Steve to get him a Bishop back. Even if she was a cousin.

This was typical of Charlie. He was, says Lis, 'such a happy man, so accepting of people' and of their ways. 'He was everyone's friend.'

Paul and Colleen helped light the path and made it a little easier for Steve and Lis. But it was still uncomfortable being sixteen and having the weight of community expectation on them.

Often Steve would duck out of school to have lunch (minimum chips with barbecue sauce) in the park with Lis. This was too much for some of the locals and occasionally a white woman would race off to the dental surgery where Lis's mother was the receptionist: 'Jenny, did you know your daughter is sitting with a blackfella?' Jenny would just smile.

The struggle made Lis and Steve's relationship all the stronger.

Things were far less complicated on the football field. Steve was making his way at representative school level and in club football.

Having played his junior footy with the Murgon Mustangs, Steve was itching to play in the seniors. He was lured across to

Wondai, half an hour up the road, by the prospect of a few dollars – beer money really. He was just as successful up against the men, and soon was playing a full game in the Under 19s and a full game in the Reserve Grade. Then he would sit on the bench for the A Grade as well, and was as keen to get out there as if he hadn't played at all. Sometimes he would be extremely frustrated at A Grade level. He always felt he could make a difference on the field – that despite his relative physical immaturity he was agile and elusive enough to look after himself.

Frankie Malone, by then a very experienced footballer with a big reputation, remembers playing against Steve in Reserve Grade for Cherbourg against Wondai. 'We were watchin' him,' he remembers. 'I was out in the centres. He got the ball and four of us went in to tackle him, to hit him. We all had him. He still got out of it. How did he get out of it? I'm still thinking today how he did it. He was just gone.'

People were starting to take notice. Paul Bishop, who usually packed down in the second row for Murgon, would often find himself in a defensive role in the centres when the Mustangs came up against Wondai, their traditional rivals. In one of those matches, a night game for the President's Cup, Steve scored five tries – against him. It was one of those moments in country sport when the players were upset they were getting thrashed but somehow respectful that they were playing against such class. Steve was unstoppable: pace, timing, and the coordination which made him appear physically stronger than he actually was. 'Bucko was the talk of the league,' Paul recalls. 'And he had this incredible knack of scoring tries.'

One weekend he scored twelve tries. But, as is Steve's way, he doesn't remember anything much about them. People were amazed. Who was this kid?

And he was just a kid. He still wasn't very big – around 180 centimetres and just 70 kilograms – and that meant he was often targeted. 'But no one got him,' Paul says.

His mother always worried. And to placate her, Steve continued to wear his headgear.

Steve was also learning the folklore of football. Wondai were sponsored by the pub at Wooroolin, a small town nearby, and the Wondai footy crowd, including the players, were often in there on a Friday night. Steve loved those days of total freedom: a million beers, and Chisel, and a lot of laughs. And the blokes. And then footy on the Sunday. All he had to do was turn up. He had no responsibilities, no commitments. What could be better? Innocent days. Carefree days. Football came easily to him.

Greg Smith continued to marvel at Steve's talent. But he was concerned that Steve wouldn't stand up to the demands of three successive days of football when he went to the national carnival in Perth. He cautioned Steve, warning him he would have to get fit. Steve was keen to play well in the carnival. 'He really wanted to make the Australian side,' Smith remembers. 'But his attitude to training hadn't improved at all.' He was often missing when the Murgon High team had a light run at lunchtime. Smith knew exactly where Steve was – down town with Lis.

Smith was right to be concerned. Steve was underdone for that Perth carnival and, as outstanding as he was, there were others who were more consistent. Local South Burnett football was of a high standard, but in Perth Steve came up against those who had greater ability; players like Brad Clyde who would go on to be top class. Steve was extremely disappointed not to make that Australian Schoolboys side.

Back in Murgon, Ed Scott, who had played rugby league for Valleys and Wests in Brisbane and ran the local YMCA, called Steve aside. He asked Steve what he wanted to do in football.

Steve replied, 'I want to play A Grade, Mr Scott.'

'That's good,' Ed said.

'Yeah, I want to play here,' Steve explained.

Ed looked him in the eye and said, 'I was thinking something a bit better than that. What about playing for Brisbane?'

Steve was more than a little surprised. And more than a little attracted by the prospect. Ed asked if he could send a letter through to the Broncos, to which Steve responded, 'Why not. I suppose we should give it a go.'

The Brisbane Broncos had just been formed, and Ed Scott (and Greg Smith) had been asked by the new club to be on the lookout for young talent in their area. The Broncos were putting together a network of scouts around Queensland, and especially around junior football, which was eventually coordinated by Cyril Connell who had played for the Maroons and had been a deputy director of education in Queensland. He was highly respected and was a factor in recruiting some of the best talent to Brisbane.

Ed Scott knew how good a player Steve Renouf could be. He was raving about the potential of the young centre. Within a couple of weeks Wayne Bennett was in Murgon, introducing himself to Steve and the Renouf family. Steve was rapt: here was a famous football identity, an Australian player and a senior coach, sitting around the kitchen table at Palmer Street having a cuppa and a good old chinwag with his mum and dad. And he was inviting Steve to come and play football.

Nerida wasn't keen on Steve going to Brisbane. Football wasn't the issue. She didn't want any of her children to leave Murgon. She was saddened by their absence. But Christine and Hazel were already in Brisbane, so at least if Steve decided to go he would have family down there.

Old Charlie could see how much his young fella wanted to give it a crack. Steve was keen and the decision wasn't too hard for him.

Lis knew nothing of what was going on. She knew he was a good footballer, but she didn't realise how good. 'He didn't tell me that clubs were interested in him,' she recalls. 'That was just Steve: he didn't talk about himself. I suddenly realised that [Steve signing on] meant we were probably going to have to part. That was a hard time. That was a really hard time.'

By August Steve Renouf was a Bronco. John Ribot, the club's general manager, went to Murgon with a three-year deal mapped out, an unusually long contract for a first-year player. This was big news in the district and Nerida and Old Charlie and Ed Scott appeared in a photo in the *South Burnett Times* watching as John Ribot showed Steve where to sign. Steve had also been approached by Newcastle and by Western Suburbs but really wanted to go to Brisbane. The *South Burnett Times* reported: 'Renouf said this was the opportunity he wanted as he was able to be involved in a team playing in the Sydney competition and at the same time be not too far away from his family.'

The *Courier-Mail* made it news all around Queensland, reporting that Steve had signed. Ribot was quoted as saying: 'Steve is more investment down the track for us. He is very excited by the prospect of being coached by Wayne Bennett and that we can do a whole package for him.'

Steve was certainly excited, but he also harboured concerns about whether he would handle top-class senior football, and whether he was doing the right thing. He copped plenty of stick in local footy once he had signed, the standard sledge being that he wasn't up to it. Some of the remarks were full of resentment.

Some of it was more playful. When Paul Bishop gave him 'a little tap on the ear' and Steve reacted, Paul turned to him and said quietly, 'If you can't take that, mate, I wouldn't be bothered turning up at the Broncos.' But even those close to him, who understood his talent and were hopeful for him, were concerned he wouldn't cope with the incessant demands of professional sport. Greg Smith wondered how he would handle the training.

Naturally Steve was excited at the prospect of entering a world which he had so revered. If things went his way he would be playing among the footballers who adorned his walls. This was fantastic – in the true sense of the word. He was about to step in to a world which in some ways existed only as fantasy, as a dream, as imagining.

So he approached his opportunity seriously. A parcel came from the Broncos addressed to Steve Renouf, 31 Palmer St, Murgon, containing Broncos' training gear and a letter explaining that whenever and wherever Steve was training he was expected to wear this gear. After that, Steve could be seen plodding along to training in Murgon in his Broncos' kit. He laughs now at how literally he took everything and how earnest he was. He was like the naive student who was the first of his family to attend university. He certainly respected the football world, and he was happy to do what it asked of him.

The Brisbane Broncos Football Club was launched at a lavish function at Government House. Steve attended the enormous public splash. He was introduced to the Governor, Sir Walter Campbell. Generally there was an atmosphere that football mattered and important and influential people from all walks of life thought it mattered as well.

Steve had mixed feelings about this. On the one hand the confident Steve Renouf was thrilled to be invited into this world. And, as Elissa says, 'He was entitled to be confident. Whatever Steve did, he did well. As long as it came easily to him.' On the other hand there was doubt in his own mind about whether he was up to it.

These tensions were strong. In many ways Steve couldn't wait to get down to Brisbane. Yet he was also very sad. He would be leaving his home town, which he loved. He would be leaving local football where he was an established star.

And he was leaving Lis.

CHAPTER 5

Apprenticeship

IT'S MARCH: Round 1 of the 1988 season. Sunday afternoon. The Brisbane Broncos versus the reigning New South Wales Rugby League premiers, Manly. All over Queensland people are wondering how the Broncos will go. Will they live up to the promises they've been making? Or will they be a big flop?

They have come together quickly as a club. The board has recruited a terrific squad of players: champions like Wally Lewis and Greg Dowling, and emerging young stars like Allan Langer, Chris Johns and Mick Hancock. At Lang Park they sit together in the sheds preparing for the game to come.

The build-up has mounted over the summer: weeks of expectation created by saturation press coverage and Queenslanders' love of rugby league. The Broncos are big news and the journalists have had plenty to report on. Some punters, driven by the maroon blood in their veins, have become instant Broncos fans. For many, the Broncos aren't just Brisbane's football team, they're an embodiment of Queensland. At the same time, some fans can't stand them. They see them as artificially created and wonder what will happen to the local Brisbane competition. They remain true to their local team or the Sydney team they've followed all their lives.

Somewhere out west a bus full of young footballers travels along the Warrego Highway towards Brisbane. It is full of young Broncos players, teenagers like John Plath, Andrew Gee and Steve Renouf, returning from St George, out near Roma. They have played Darling Downs–South West Queensland the night before. Wayne Bennett has implemented a youth policy. It's not just an idea: he actually believes it's the way to go. He is taking young players who show a bit of natural talent and developing them himself, making the sort of footballer he thinks will serve the club well. And he has sent them to the bush as part of their education.

There had been a good crowd at St George. They juggled beers and steakburgers, fighting the barbecue sauce as it ran down their wrists. And they saw the young Broncos turn it on.

Now the footballers sit in tired bodies listening to the commentary. They laugh and cheer as the players they've spent the summer running up hills with, some of the biggest names in rugby league, demolish the reigning premiers 44–10.

It's a great day for the Broncos, a great day for Brisbane, a great day for Queensland.

It had taken nearly six months to get there.

Steve Renouf finished high school in mid-November 1987, by coincidence the very day before he had to go to Brisbane for the first-ever Broncos training camp. That meant he had to leave early in the morning after his high school graduation. As important a moment as his first day at the Broncos was, he wasn't keen to let something like the prospect of a professional football career interfere with his high school celebrations.

The formal part of graduation night was followed by a raucous party at Brett Plowman's place, where the senior class of Murgon High School went out in style. Steve was up all night, and in outstanding partying form.

In the morning, having not slept at all, he was driven by his parents to Broncos headquarters at Wests Juniors in Brisbane. It was a difficult trip for his mother, even though she knew this wasn't the final move to Brisbane for her Bucko. He would be returning to Murgon a few days later, at least for a while.

From the Broncos headquarters he travelled to Kooralbyn with Billy Noke and Chris Johns who had both joined Brisbane from the Dragons. They made the young man feel very welcome. Chris Johns remembers him as 'a skinny little kid with big raps on him out of Murgon'.

At the Kooralbyn Valley resort Steve found himself among some of the very best players of their generation. He was introduced to all of them: to Lewis and Dowling and Miles. It was odd enough to be around them, but to be calling them Wally and GD and Geno was quite bizarre.

There were others like him, just kids, and Steve was thankful that he knew a few of their faces. Some of his Queensland Schoolboys' team-mates had signed with the Broncos and it was like a reunion of old friends: Andrew Gee, Alan Cann, Craig Teevan and John Plath (whom he knew from Wide Bay juniors).

The squad was soon hard at it. Steve was rather shell-shocked. He quickly discovered that a big night on the booze wasn't the ideal preparation for top-level rugby league training. 'I was way up the back,' he remembers. 'But I didn't feel so bad because there was Wally and GD beside me. I thought, "I can't be going too bad".'

They were pushed all day. And then they played hard at night. The older blokes stuck together and didn't have much to say to the younger ones. And the young fellas just kept thinking how great it was to be knocking around with the stars – and the grog was free as well.

Steve got through the demanding program with his reputation intact, but only just. On one 10-kilometre run he found himself with the stragglers yet again. He, John Plath and Greg Hogarth walked most of the second 5 kilometres. But for some reason Steve decided to jog up the very last hill, the first time he'd broken into a trot for some time. As it turned out, it was a judicious move. He arrived at the top of the steep incline, exhausted, to find Wayne Bennett applauding his effort, telling him he'd go a long way, and generally making him feel like a rugby league player. Then the coach looked down at the walkers and shouted, 'Get back down there, you lazy bastards. What do you think this is?'

There wasn't a lot of opportunity for Bennett to speak one-on-one with his players at that camp, although on a few occasions he chatted briefly with Steve, just offering a few words of encouragement.

Bennett spoke long and hard to the group as a whole, though. He had already won recognition as a coach – at Souths in Brisbane, at Canberra, and as the successful Queensland coach in the 1987 State of Origin series. That was enough for the Broncos board to go after him. He hadn't attained the guru status conferred on him today, but he did have ideas about teams and people and human nature, and he had plans, big plans.

Steve had never been in so many talks and so many meetings. He was absolutely knackered and just kept nodding off – arguably not the best way of making a favourable impression. In his waking moments he wondered whether he had made the right decision. 'I knew it was going to be tough,' he remembers thinking, 'but I knew I had to find a way to get through it.' For Steve, football wasn't about talking and theorising and explaining, nor about pushing his body to the limits. It was about having the ball in your hands, and playing.

He survived the camp.

Back in Murgon, he was on top of the world. Driving down the main street in the family Falcon he noticed Clint and stopped slap-bang in the middle of the street. Clint came to the passenger window and leaned in. Steve, with one hand on the wheel and the other arm across the seat, looked at him and said, 'What's happenin', bro?' A couple of cars pulled up behind him and tooted. He didn't care. He was beaming. He was as happy as Clint had ever seen him.

During that summer Steve travelled down to Brisbane many times, with his sisters or his parents. After one Broncos' session the players went off to have a few beers – again. Steve was inside St Paul's Tavern with his team-mates while his mum and dad sat outside in the car just around the corner from Boundary Street.

But the day came when Steve had to move to Brisbane permanently. This was for real. His mother was more than just sad. She was heartbroken – it was like the tearing of flesh.

It was a tough day for Lis as well. She and Steve said their farewells, confident that distance would not change how they felt.

Steve left Murgon on the Sunday of the Australia Day long weekend in 1988. He left in a state of confusion – confident and expectant, yet at the same time apprehensive and fearful. 'What am I doing?' he thought. There were voices of encouragement: people who believed in his immense talent, like his family, especially Old Charlie and Steve Button, and Greg Smith. But there were always other voices in the district: 'He'll be back inside six months', 'He won't hack it', 'He's just another blackfella wasting his time'. The same old chorus of prejudices.

When he got to Brisbane, Steve worked out he'd mixed up the

dates and had arrived a day early. The following morning his sisters were driving to Murgon, so he jumped in the car with them and headed straight back home. It was a surprise for Lis. They spent the day together at the Fick's Crossing Fun Day. But it meant they had to say goodbye again.

It made them realise how difficult it was going to be.

There were those who thought their relationship would fizzle out; that distance and the demands of everyday life would be enough to put an end to what some thought of as an awkward situation. But the early signs suggested otherwise. They spoke on the phone every second day (which was as often as Lis was allowed to). And Lis visited whenever she could – catching the bus, and getting lifts down with friends.

Throughout that first year Steve lived with his sister Christine, who was a public servant in the Aboriginal Affairs department, and her friend Robyn, in a little house in Greenslopes. When Lis was in Brisbane the young couple made the most of their time together. Her parents had asked that she stay with her Aunty Margaret in Moorooka, a request she honoured.

Steve was glad to have Hazel and Christine in Brisbane. They looked after him, cooking and helping where they could. It was important to Steve that they were just around. And that he knew they were around. It was also important that he felt he was within striking distance of Murgon and his family. Still, he found it hard.

The Broncos also looked out for him. Steve had signed his contract on John Ribot's assurance that the Broncos would help him become established in Brisbane. They found him a position as an apprentice electrician at the Mater Hospital.

Steve knew he had natural talent, but at 17 he sometimes asked himself, 'Can I make it as a rugby league player? Can I play rugby league professionally? Will that be enough to provide for a family?' Having a family was a big priority for Steve. He came from a house full of people and he wanted to fill his own house with a wife and a stack of children. To do that he had to have a good, steady income.

Steve's first contract with the Broncos was for $2000 (for each of the three years), plus a yearly bonus if he played at least five Reserve Grade games, plus win bonuses. It obviously wasn't enough to live on, so he would need something to fall back on. Playing football was something he loved, and if he could earn a little out of it, that would be a bonus. The apprenticeship at the Mater Hospital seemed, at that time, to offer a more certain future.

Steve's new life was hectic. He had had very few commitments in Murgon. He had turned up to school when he wanted to, which he usually did because he liked the social side of it. He turned up to football training when he felt like it. He went wherever he liked. No one needed to know where he was. In fact, in a house of twelve children it was impossible for Nerida to keep tabs on them all.

Now he was forced into a life of strict routine. He worked all day learning to be an electrician and then had to get across town to training. That meant catching a bus into the city, another bus to Red Hill, and then walking down the hill from Waterworks Road to the Broncos. After training he caught two buses home. It was exhausting. It all felt like work more than anything else, and he hated that feeling.

He enjoyed the company of his young team-mates, but he found the senior players quite aloof. They had their own friendships – like the Wynnum connection of Lewis, Miles, Dowling and Scott – and tended to stick together. To Steve they seemed quite separate and unapproachable. But Steve was very shy and unlikely to seek them out. 'I'm not a big talker now,' he says, 'and I was even worse then.'

Often he wondered why he was bothering with football. It didn't seem to be the same game he'd loved so much at home. He would ring Lis, physically exhausted and almost defeated: 'I can't do this.' 'I miss you.' 'I want to come home.' Sometimes he was in tears. He was sad and lonely.

The tonic for Steve was to head home to Murgon. He considered injuries something of a blessing. As soon as he had a physical problem he'd race back to Lis and Murgon and Palmer Street. Football was full of contradictions for Steve. He liked it, but he didn't like it.

Wayne Bennett knew Steve Renouf was going to be an unusual player to nurture. He knew that it was going to take time. But from the first time he saw him he knew he would be working with a supremely talented athlete. 'I could see his great ability to run,' Wayne Bennett recalls. 'His balance was everything. He had the ability to accelerate from nothing to great speed in a very short time. These were his great strengths. The rest I knew he would have to work for.'

Steve's liabilities were obvious to Bennett: 'He wasn't a great defensive player, he didn't have a great attitude to training, and he'd never been in a weights room in his life.'

Bennett understood the sort of footballer Steve was: a gifted player for whom things had come very easily, and that meant he had never had to learn the elements of the game. He could see Steve was, by instinct and by nature, an attacking player who was a less than active defender. His speed had always compensated for his technical inadequacies. It would take a lot of work to overcome his prejudice against the defensive side of the game. In many ways he was a typical Bronco. Players headed onto Lang Park believing they could score from anywhere, and Steve certainly had known that feeling at home.

In that 1988 season the younger players were assigned to local

Brisbane Rugby League clubs and Steve went to Davies Park where he played mainly in Souths' Colts. He performed extremely well in a competition where he was still able to stand out. The football was of a fair standard, but Steve recalls thinking that his junior side in Murgon, which won four successive premierships under Steve Button, would have been a pretty good chance to beat his Souths side.

Steve was making good progress. He attributes much of his early success to Billy Gardiner, whose role at the Broncos was to help look after the younger players. Gardiner helped him as a footballer and gave him sound advice about fitting all the pieces of his busy life together. 'Billy looked out for me,' Steve recalls. 'He was always there for a chat. He was a builder and he'd pick me up in his ute and drive me down to training, and that's when we'd chat. Nothing was too much trouble for Billy.'

Occasionally Steve had a run with the seniors at Souths. He also trained with the Broncos Reserve Grade. He really stood out – just in the way he moved. Brook Kennedy could see how classy he was. In fact Steve reminded Kennedy of the black Englishman Ellery Hanley, who was playing with Balmain. Hanley was known as 'Pearl'. So, in that half-joking, half-serious way of a football club, Kennedy started calling Steve 'Pearl'. If there were traces of irony in the nickname, there were also traces of respect. Steve had the potential to turn out like another Ellery Hanley. He could be another 'Pearl', and very little of what he did over the next decade prompted anyone to challenge the name. In those early days, some players called him Susan (after Sydney socialite Susan Renouf), but most called him Pearl. It became his Broncos name, and it stuck.

During that season Steve twice sat on the bench for the Broncos Reserve Grade, the first time on a cold day at Cronulla. It was no great debut. When he finally came on for a run on the wing, he was overwhelmed by the pace of the game. He reckons he 'did nothing but run out of puff'. It made him feel he had a long way to go.

The imagination can accentuate differences though. That day the Broncos Reserve Grade team sat on the ground by the gate waiting for the First Graders to come out of the sheds. He remembers the slick Sharks' players prancing past, shining with linament: 'To me at that time, I thought these guys were just massive – ET and Mark McGaw. Now I know they aren't really.' Steve was clearly nervous about senior footy.

Steve's excellent form with Souths' Colts saw him selected for the City Under 18 side. In a happy coincidence City was scheduled to take on Wide Bay – at Murgon. So the young star had an early home-coming, playing against many of his former team-mates. The whole scenario made him wonder, yet again, about his decision to leave his home town.

Yet it was a memorable occasion for Steve playing at the show-grounds just metres from Palmer Street, in front of his family and friends. And there was a terrific sense of mutual respect and camaraderie after the game when he mingled with the Wide Bay players. It would have been easy to stay there.

During that season Steve played in the Queensland Under 18 side, captained by Andrew Gee, which beat New South Wales 8–4 in Sydney. But later, Souths' Colts were knocked out in the semifinals. And footy was over for the season.

Not that Steve was too worried. He had more important things on his mind. After a season of living apart, Lis decided she would move to Brisbane. She continued her hairdressers' apprenticeship at Zorba's Hair Fashions in the Carindale Shopping Centre. She lived with her aunt.

Lis and Steve soon became engaged so they could live together, deflecting the criticism they were too young to get married (and the usual home-town taunts, 'She must be pregnant'). They knew how they felt and that they wanted to build a life together. There was no stopping Lis.

They were like many other young couples. It was a bit of a financial struggle. They rented a flat at Annerley, and managed to keep the silver Gemini in approximately roadworthy condition, and when the cheque came from the Broncos at the end of the season they added to their few items of furniture.

Steve was very much the ordinary, everyday apprentice electrician who played football. He still thought like an amateur. He wasn't Steve Renouf, footballer. Others were sure that one day he would be. Chris Johns thought it was just a matter of time. 'Everyone just kept talking about this kid who was scoring tries,' he remembers of that season. 'We knew he could play. There were plenty of centres around [at the Broncos] then, but even still we knew that it wouldn't be long before he was putting pressure on the established players.'

The question was whether Steve could believe it himself.

After another arduous pre-season, Steve started the 1989 premiership season in Reserve Grade. He had won no accolades for his approach to fitness work but he continued to show a ton of ability on the football field. People were noticing him. He had that something, that fluid movement that attracts the eye. He had a knack for making breaks and getting the ball over the line. Against Manly he won the match for the Broncos in the dying minutes. The *Courier-Mail* reported: 'Young centre Steve Renouf added to his growing reputation with a dazzling 25 metre solo try.' There were other impressive early season performances.

But what changes a footballer's sense of himself? What helps him to believe he can play? That he has a future in the game? Steve Renouf was just eighteen and he wasn't sure about his ability. What was a mention in a newspaper worth?

He wasn't feeling confident at all, and then one day, just weeks into the season, Wayne Bennett had a quiet word to him. 'Steve,' he said, 'you play that well I can't keep you out of the first grade side.' Steve got a huge lift. 'Those words,' he says, 'stuck in my head throughout my career.'

With a number of senior Broncos on Test duty, Steve was picked for his first Winfield Cup match in Round 4. 'Murgon Marvel Scores Call-Up', announced the *Courier-Mail*. 'Lazy Steve given run with firsts', said the *Sun*. For the next couple of days he was everywhere in the papers. The headline to Alfie Langer's *Daily Mirror* column claimed, 'He's the worst trainer since Wally' and 'Slow-coach Steve fires on the field'. A small photo was captioned, 'Straggler: Renouf'. Alfie wrote:

> Steve Renouf, the Broncos' newly-promoted winger, is being hailed as a try-scoring genius. But as far as training is concerned he's pretty much in the no-hoper class. It's a big statement I know but Steve is an even worse trainer than the so-called King of the Stragglers, Wally Lewis. Renouf just doesn't like exerting himself in non-match situations.

Errol Harris continued the comparison with Lewis, but in a more positive sense: 'Like Lewis,' he wrote, 'when it comes to playing the game, Renouf's natural ability overshadows his training trait.'

On the same day the *Courier-Mail* published Steve Gray's short profile with a photo of Steve in his work-gear at the Mater Hospital. The articles kept coming. He was an 'exciting prospect', a 'teenage sensation' and a 'prolific try-scorer', the story of his twelve-try weekend in Murgon being told and retold. *The Big League* reported that even Wayne Bennett 'nominated Steve Renouf as the club's laziest trainer'.

On the television news the announcement of his selection was accompanied by a number of profiles as well. Pat Welsh explained that Steve had 'heard of his selection through a congratulatory call from his girlfriend's parents'. Steve's first-ever television interview was with Channel 7's Bill McDonald, who described him as 'a shy youngster'. He was also modest. Filmed at work, and resplendent in his electricians kit and a very well-kept mullet, Steve said in a quiet and gentle voice, 'I didn't think I'd be up there this early. I'll give it my best and see what happens.'

Channel 9 was more upbeat. Sports presenter Allan Thomas, who knew a crook horse, a fair boxer, and a talented rugby league footballer, said, 'The boy from Murgon has been playing sensationally in Reserve Grade and is a lot fitter this year.' An interview followed during which Steve assured Queenslanders that he was a better trainer than his team-mates thought. 'I found it hard just adjusting to the training because coming from the bush we didn't train that hard up there,' he said earnestly. 'This year I've really got a hold of it.'

Suddenly Steve was in the public gaze. Here was a young man, still unsure of his own ability, being built up as the next new star. People were asking, 'Who is this Aboriginal kid we've been hearing about?' That put the pressure on him, which shouldn't be underestimated. We take it for granted that footballers, however young they might be, will walk into top-level football and be able to perform as we expect them to. If they don't, we see it as our divine right to bag them. It's one of the many reasons we follow football. We love being armchair critics.

It was a big week for Steve, even before he boarded the plane to Sydney. On a grey sort of day, Orana Park was a mushy-wet football field. Steve sat quietly in the dressing rooms. He was understandably tense. 'The boys were great,' he remembers. 'They just said, "Do what you do".'

He remembers vividly Bennett coming over and giving him a typical Bennett talk. 'It's a settling talk,' he says of Bennett's style.

'It's not a pressure talk. It's not a pep-talk. He's not pumping you up. That's what's so good about him. He made me feel secure about going out there. He just said, "You've got all the other guys around you. They're there for you. Don't do anything different: just go out and play".'

It seemed Wayne Bennett already knew what was at the heart of his young player. 'Play' was the right word. It was play that motivated Steve Renouf.

Steve trotted onto the field: a young footballer with a boofy, 1980s haircut. He really did look like a schoolboy. He knew he was in full public view, and yet there were moments when he was in a world of his own out there, so naive that he wasn't overawed. On the one hand it was just another game of football. On the other hand it had the grandeur of something he'd followed and watched and worked towards for some time. Playing on the wing he fielded a lot of kicks in the poor conditions and performed honestly. His moment came when called on in defence. Wests half-back Trevor Cogger looked like running the length of the field to score, when Renouf came from nowhere to mow him down. It was a match-saving tackle from the young speedster.

He continued to attract attention and comment. In the Wednesday night Panasonic Cup match against Parramatta in Townsville he scored two tries in the Broncos 42–6 win. It was the way he scored them that had people noticing him; the way he moved, his poise, his acceleration. He was being groomed as a replacement for Tony Currie, and with representative football taking some of the top Broncos away he was given further opportunities.

Not all went smoothly against Manly, though. By his own admission, he was having an absolute shocker when one of his senior team-mates had a go at him. Chris Johns remembers the incident clearly:

Steve just wasn't having a good game. I could see he was shattered. Now Greg Dowling's no Henry Kissinger; he's no master of diplomacy. I remember him sticking his head out of the scrum and yelling, 'Get that kid off this field'. GD's a real competitor and Steve had let a few tries in, but I thought, 'Geez, that's nice', so I went over to Steve and said, 'Don't worry, he says that to everyone, mate.' It was a pretty tough baptism. That was probably the only time I went out of my way. I just told him to take it with a grain of salt and to just do what you do best.

Dowling's remark was a pivotal moment in Steve's career, and an incident remembered by many. Here he was, a young man challenged openly by a team-mate. If anything made him question where he was, and what he was doing, it was that sort of unfettered criticism. Did he belong in first grade rugby league? It was a testing time: he could wilt and take off, or he could stay and fight and prove himself.

The doubts seemed to multiply. There were doubts about his defence. There were doubts about his training and his fitness. And sometimes there were doubts about his ball-handling. It seemed that every time his parents were in the crowd he couldn't hang on to anything. That had to be addressed. So Old Charlie and Nerida wouldn't tell Steve when they were coming down to Brisbane.

But Wayne Bennett had faith in Steve's ability. 'When I saw what he could do,' he says, 'I just had a long-term plan. I was prepared to teach him how to tackle, to get that part right. Getting him training better. Getting the process right . . . I knew there was something there. That's why I'm the coach. I've just got to hold my nerve when everyone else says it won't work.' The Dowling incident was significant. 'There was one game he played when a player on the field suggested he should get off the field,' Bennett remembers. 'That upset me greatly. I addressed that issue in another way later on. There were some players who questioned him but I said to them, "This is what he needs and I know he's going to make it".'

Bennett had patience. Steve wasn't sure himself of what was expected of a top-class rugby league player. In some ways he was so different, so unaffected, that he appeared oblivious to that expectation. He was just himself. But if he was going to make it, he had to understand those expectations. It would take time, time that Bennett was willing to give him. 'Every time he trained that bit harder and went that bit further at training and played that bit harder on match day and got a bit of confidence about himself he was growing as a person,' Bennett explains. 'I wanted to keep that process going. There were a lot of things he wasn't doing, but I didn't dwell on them. That wasn't going to help him as a person. Criticism never helped Steve Renouf.'

Some of his team-mates had less patience than the coach, and Steve was certainly talked about by the senior players. They weren't as quick to understand Steve's nature. Tony Currie remembers: 'I said to Wayne, "What about this bloke?" And Wayne would just say, "Don't worry. You'll owe me." We knew the kid could play. But Wayne said to me, "I'll give a bit here but I reckon I'll get a bit more out of him in the end".'

There were flashes of sheer brilliance which helped convince the doubters. Two incidents will stay in Currie's memory forever. The first was in the Broncos 42–10 defeat of Cronulla at Lang Park in June 1989. It was the weekend after State of Origin and Currie was one of the few players to back up. Steve had a blinder. The *Courier-Mail* described him as running 'rampant' in the back-line. Currie remembers Steve getting the ball just out from the Broncos' own line:

I was just standing there watchin' and thinkin', how good is this bloke? Steve got it 15 metres off our line. He swerved to beat the first and took off, quick, real quick, down the left-hand wing. I'll never forget it – heading towards the Fourex end. He bumped off the full-back. That allowed the cover to get there and just as they got to him he fended with his right hand and got a one-handed ball, left hand, across his body, perfectly timed, to Gary French who went in under the posts. I'm standin' 50 metres away shaking my head: 93 skills in a split second going at even time. And then he doesn't say a word. Not a word.

Currie saw what Bennett saw, but he wasn't sure Steve could improve in those other areas. But other moments convinced Currie it was worth a try. 'I'll never forget the day he stood up Phil Blake,' Currie says. 'Blake had been in the game a long time. He knew what he could do. He knew his opposition. Blake was a real professional. He was at the peak of his career. And this kid Renouf just went neeerh, neeeerh, neeeerh and I looked up and went, "This kid's special".'

Not everyone was convinced. The punters were getting stuck in. Pub conversations about Steve Renouf were along the lines of: 'He can be brilliant in attack.' Sip. 'But his defence is shit-house.' Sip. Sip. They were right. His defence, particularly against opponents with any size to them, was suspect. Although he had worked on his weight and strength, he was still an immature 81 kilograms. Some footballers play above their weight. But, if anything, Steve looked lighter, as if he could be easily tossed around.

When both Chris Johns and Tony Currie were unavailable for the match against Canterbury in July, Renouf and Peter Jackson were named in the centres. The *Courier-Mail*'s Steve Ricketts pointed out Renouf was 'in the hot seat'. He would be marking Andrew Farrar, as hard a centre as there was going around. Canterbury won the game at Belmore, 22–8.

The rumblings grew louder. The doubts festered. In a later newspaper profile of Steve, Bennett is quoted as saying, 'I ended up asking John [Ribot] to tell the Broncos board not to listen to all the whingeing going on about Steve. I sent the word up the line that this kid was going to win us a lot more games than he was going to lose us.'

Steve finished the season in Reserve Grade, scoring three tries to help his team win their play-off for fifth place. But the arduous program caught up with the young Broncos and they went down to Canberra 22–14, a match in which Steve scored two more tries. In fact he was the club's leading try-scorer that season, equalling Lewis's record of fifteen from the previous year. That's what Steve Renouf was becoming known for: scoring tries. But not one of them was scored in his ten First Grade appearances.

The jury was still out on the young Steve Renouf.

CHAPTER 6

Struggle

S TEVE AND LIS were married in the Uniting Church at Murgon on 24 February 1990. They were both nineteen years old. It was a traditional ceremony followed by a reception under a marquee on 'Silverleaf'. It was a happy celebration, although some thought they were very young to be getting married, and were worried about the cultural differences.

At the end of the night, when it was time to bid the bride and groom farewell, Steve and Lis put on white overalls and were given caps with miner's lights on them. They were helped into a canoe and, waving goodbye to the wedding guests, they paddled up the creek into the honeymoon night. They splashed and laughed their way to a natural island, a spot which Lis loved. She had always said she wanted to camp there some time. It had been raining, but every effort had been made to have the honeymoon suite – a tent – ready for them. Unfortunately, the official assemblers of the suite had forgotten the pump for the airbed. And there were bats. And Steve was petrified of the dark, 'like a real blackfella', as Lis would say. Still, there they were, on their wedding night, on their own little island.

In the days that followed they honeymooned in Hervey Bay, where it rained and rained. So they returned to Murgon for a few days before heading back to Brisbane.

It was a time of optimism and opportunity. Steve hoped to nail down a spot in First Grade and Lis continued working at Zorba's.

They had a busy routine; by Steve's standards it was hectic. He was away a lot – at training or travelling to games interstate – and Lis missed him terribly. They were happiest at home together, or having a quiet bite at the nearby Chinese restaurant. Steve wasn't one to talk about football much but Lis could sense when it was getting hard for him. That's when she was at her best. She was blessed with an inner resolve far beyond her years – a stoicism that life on the land can bring. She kept things going. She wanted Steve to make it in football, to show the world what he could do. So as soon as Steve showed signs of slackening off, she was onto him. When he wanted to miss work or training, she wouldn't hear of it.

Steve continued his apprenticeship at the Mater Hospital, where he got on well with the other electricians. They had a lot of time for him. Sure he was on tele, and half-famous, and could get them tickets to Broncos games. But in the routine of daily work that was almost forgotten. In the workshop the blokes – especially John Hunter and John McKew – really got to know and like Steve, and wanted the best for him. They liked that he was unaffected by the success he was having on the footy field and the public notoriety he attracted.

It was like any other workplace: whatever it takes to get you through the day. They'd sometimes go down to the Stone's Corner pub after work and have a couple of beers. Steve was a capable apprentice, a good worker who understood his limitations. 'His attitude to work was pretty good,' Hunter remembers. 'He got the job done. But he always took shortcuts; always the easiest way, never the hard way.'

His workmates called him Bucko, a name which consistently affirmed his Aboriginal self. They knew he was proud of his heritage. He didn't talk about it much, but there were times when he made it clear he was a Murri. On one occasion Steve and John were doing a job in the pharmacy. Everyone at the hospital – in fact, just about everyone north of the Tweed – knew who the emerging footballer was. The pharmacist, trying to wind Steve up, asked, 'So what part of Europe are you from?' Steve looked at her and said, 'I'm Aboriginal,' then turned and walked away.

He also painted a large Aboriginal flag on the drawers of his desk, without saying anything. The boys didn't need to say anything either – they knew it was just part of Steve.

The Mater was pleased to have a top footballer working in the hospital. Steve often stopped by the wards to visit the patients, especially the children, to help cheer them up. It came very naturally to him. He was regularly in the hospital newsletter and the occasional photo in the newspapers was good publicity for the hospital. Management was happy to give him the time off he needed (and he occasionally took a bit more). He was supposed to make the time up, but he never quite did. One day Steve reckoned he needed a couple of hours at the physio, so off he went. The boys were working away in the workshop when across the radio came, 'And if you're after Steve Renouf's autograph, he's here at Toombul Shoppingtown right now.'

His workmates could tell when the physical demands of his twin existence were catching up with him. 'He didn't mind having a sleep,' Hunter chuckles. In the early years they knew how much he hated training – all aspects of training. He used to complain about having to put on bulk. Often he would turn up to work sore and proppy. But he certainly wasn't a complainer. And they

Steve's Dad, Old Charlie, and Mum, Nerida, at Steve
and Elissa's wedding in 1990.

Steve's maternal grandmother,
Nan South, with Steve and Lis at
their wedding.

Surrounded by sisters: Steve was the
tenth child in the family. The five
around him were girls. Here he is
with (from left) Christine, Colleen,
Sonia and Angela.

Steve playing for Murgon Under 17s against Nanango at Murgon. A rare shot: Steve actually passing a football!

The old wooden grandstand at Murgon where the crowd would get rather boisterous. Steve played most of his junior football at this ground.
(*South Burnett Times*)

Steve signs his first Broncos contract. Old Charlie and Nerida look on proudly. Ed Scott, then director of the local YMCA, was instrumental in introducing the Renoufs to his old friend John Ribot, and the rest is history. (*South Burnett Times*, June 1986)

Steve, a vital cog in the enormous machine that is the Mater Hospital. Pictured here, in the late 1980s, in his electrician's gear in the workshop. (*Courier-Mail*)

Part of the Renouf family with Steve and Lis on their wedding day, February 1990. (*Courier-Mail*)

Newlyweds: Steve and Lis re-create their honeymoon night. When they were farewelled from the reception on the Bishop family property, they paddled up the creek to an island where they spent a memorable night in the honeymoon tent. (*Courier-Mail*)

Steve and Lis, shortly before the exciting series of events of late 1992: the Grand Final victory against St George, the World Cup win in England, and the birth of their first child, Sam, on December 3. (*Sunday Mail*, Peter McNamara)

Steve and Lis and Sam outside 31 Palmer St, the Renouf family home, a real gathering place for the Renoufs. (*Courier-Mail*, Sandra Priestley)

Steve with baby Sam: a classic photograph which caught the attention of everyone from mums and dads, football fans, and even academics. (*Courier-Mail*, Geoff McLachlan)

Making an impression. A young Steve, running at his boyhood hero Mal Meninga, against Canberra in 1991. After this match Mal predicted a big future for the emerging star.

A great moment for any team: 1992 premiers and ready to celebrate.
(Action Photographs)

Steve snags the winning try for Australia against Great Britain at Wembley in 1992. All credit, says Steve, to a persistent Kevvy Walters and his brilliant outball. Suddenly, it seemed, everyone knew who Steve Renouf was. (Action Photographs)

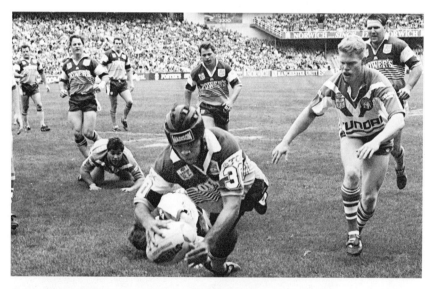

Some comeback. Steve returns to football, after his jaw injury, for the 1993 preliminary final, and scores with his first touch. The Broncos beat Canterbury 23-16 at the Sydney Football Stadium to take their place in the Grand Final. (*Courier-Mail*, Jim Fenwick)

What flexibility and balance!
Almost collared. Keeps his feet.
Then the characteristic Renouf
dive: nothing extravagant and ball
carefully protected. One of three
tries in the 40–10 win over Souths
at ANZ Stadium, in 1994.
(*Courier-Mail*, Geoff McLachlan)

knew he was intent on finishing his apprenticeship properly. He thought he might need his ticket. As good as his progress had been as a young player at the Broncos, there was that ever-nagging question: could he make it as a professional footballer?

Some Broncos fans were a little disappointed with their team's performances in the first two seasons in the competition. The player list boasted international and Origin stars, and many supporters thought that just one finals appearance – the 1989 loss to Cronulla – was not a satisfactory outcome.

When Canterbury premiership player Tony Currie arrived at the Broncos at the start of the club's second year he thought the fledgling football club was in pretty good shape. But he noted two main differences: training had been much harder in Sydney, and the Canterbury coaching staff had paid far more attention to defensive skills. At Belmore, attack and defence were treated equally. At the Broncos, Currie was surprised to find that the ratio 'was about 80/20'. Many of the senior Broncos had come out of the Brisbane Rugby League competition where attitudes to training were comparatively lackadaisical, and a similar culture was growing at the Broncos. This was a concern for the club hierarchy.

A new training regime was put in place and, if Steve had found the previous summer tough, this pre-season was even more demanding. The club appointed Kelvin Giles, a physical trainer with a background in the British Army, and experience working with the British Olympic athletics team, who was determined to give the Broncos a fitness edge over their rivals. He barked orders. It was his job to make the players run, and when they weren't running, to have them labouring in the gym.

You forget how hard footballers work; how hard they are expected to push themselves. While we're at the beach, they're running up sandhills and doing 400s in the heat and the humidity of a Queensland January. Steve hated it. There was something deep inside him that even made him fear it; some force difficult to explain. It was not really laziness – although he could be lazy – but an apprehension; a reticence. As if it wasn't worth putting himself through the pain. As if the demands were almost inhuman or unnatural. It was a simple choice for Steve: if a person has the choice of pain or no-pain, it seemed reasonable to choose the no-pain option. And Wayne Bennett understood that. 'Steve told me in later years,' Bennett recalls, 'and I knew it had happened, that from lunchtime he would be sick thinking about training and what he would have to go through. Most blokes go through that, but not to the same degree. For Steve it was a real issue.'

If Steve knew there was a torrid training afternoon planned, he would be nervous. Training might be a dozen or so 400s at effort with a one-and-a-half-minute break between them, or 400s with shuttle runs in between, or just constant work. He especially hated having to run against the clock, because he found it harder to push himself. He would panic. He hated the incessant testing. He couldn't see why it was necessary when everyone had been doing the work, and the trainers had seen them doing the work.

It really worried him, and Steve was notoriously a bloke who didn't worry about much. He didn't know how much to eat. If he didn't eat enough he'd feel weak; if he ate too much he'd be head on hands on the fence close to throwing up. When he got to training, the pain he anticipated always arrived. Without fail. And as much as he tried not to let it, it would upset him. Close to tears at times, the same question weighed on him, 'Why do we have to do this? This is bullshit.' Training was only good when it was over. 'I was like a bottle of red,' Steve admits. 'It took me a long time to mature. I didn't catch the point of training until much later in my career: that when you were physically and mentally tired in a game, you drew on that reserve you'd developed at training.'

It wasn't in Steve's nature to push himself to do something. If he could do it, he would. If he couldn't, he'd do something else. Tony Currie wasn't much of a trainer either. 'I was a shocker,' he confesses, 'but Steve was even behind me. I could always count on beating The Pearl in a 400.'

Giles knew a good athlete when he saw one, and he was wise to blokes like Tony Currie and Steve Renouf. He knew they wouldn't exert themselves, that they were classic middle-of-the-packers, just trying to keep out of view. So he instituted the rabbit run. He'd pick out two players to be rabbits: say Steve and TC. They would start 15 metres in front of the pack of hounds (the rest of the players). The hounds would chase, trying to catch the rabbits, over 400 metres. For every hound who beat the rabbits to the finish line, the rabbits would have to do an extra 400 after training. If five hounds got past, there were five additional 400s to be run before the player could hit the showers. Steve and Tony never got beaten. They could hear the footsteps. Giles would laugh. 'I knew you had it in you,' he'd say. It was a matter of extracting it from them.

The press noticed a change in Steve's attitude to training, if not in his actual training performance. He was photographed with weights and on the track, and was interviewed about his transformation. 'My overall commitment to training is totally different to last year,' he told the Brisbane *Sun*. But training remained a battle for him.

Lis kept on encouraging him – even pushing him – insisting he keep plugging away. 'Lis was really important,' Bennett explains. 'She was a stabiliser. She was at one end; I was at the other end.' And slowly Steve Renouf started to believe that not only was it worth it but that he could actually get through it. The prospect of playing top football was becoming an increasingly significant motivator.

It was happening slowly. 'I don't think there was a single defining moment in Steve's career,' Bennett observes. 'Getting him to training was a defining moment, then getting him to finish training was another. We named the hill after him because he spent so much time sitting on it. But we accepted all those things. I saw other Aboriginal boys turn up and they just disappeared on us, but he kept coming back.'

Steve was supported by those close to him, but his own resolve should not be underestimated. 'I wanted to prove to myself that I could play football at the top level,' he explains. 'And sometimes I thought of it as my job. It was what I was paid to do.' At that stage, payment didn't make it any easier. But despite the temptation of the easy option, he did stick with it.

It is hard to know how much a person's cultural heritage impacts on his life – whether Steve had the attitudes he had *because* he was a Murri. It's hard to know what is a cultural trait, and what is a personal trait. It's hard to give words to the complex way these two concepts are linked. Bennett is careful to look at the individual person, but is willing to make more general statements as well. 'I know the Aboriginal boys are different and I try to treat them a bit differently – and yet the same. They're very much confidence people. They come to a big club like this, they've got to feel you care about them. I always hoped that's how Steve felt: that I felt for him, that I cared about him.'

Professional rugby league, however, is played on white man's terms. Mainstream Australian culture values success and achievement. People build reputations because of their success. Reputations matter, therefore success matters. Victory counts. The team counts. Commitment to the team counts. Consistency counts. These values are taken for granted. They are so ingrained in the culture that they are seen as the natural way, and often the *only* way.

By contrast, spasmodically brilliant individual performance, while thrilling to watch, is not regarded as an end in itself in the professional sports culture. It might be regarded so in Cherbourg rugby league culture, in schoolyard touch footy culture, in Top End Australian rules football culture, in the street basketball culture of some African Americans. But it is not regarded as such at the elite level of rugby league in Australia. Playing, however brilliantly, is not enough. Winning matters. And in mainstream Australian sport that means discipline and hard work.

Some players enter the world of professional rugby league with an attitude to their own performance which may rub their coaches up the wrong way. It's not that their attitude is wrong, it is that it is *different*. Often there is a tension between the player who wants to perform – to take the high-risk option, to throw the speculative pass, to produce the chip-and-chase on the second tackle – and the coach's demand for low-risk options.

Steve arrived at the Broncos a performer. Rugby league was about having the footy in his hands and showing what he could do with it. It was about performing the skills which came naturally to him; skills he didn't have to work for; skills which were just in him; skills which in some way were related to who he was. This was the way he had always enjoyed his football. It was going to be tough for Steve to fall into line with a professional football culture. It wasn't just a matter of making a few minor adjustments; it required profound changes in his approach to football, in his approach to life, in his sense of himself.

The question for Steve Renouf was whether he was willing to put some of the elements of his identity to the side, to alter them, in some senses quite significantly, to become the professional footballer others believed he could be. The situation was made more complex because he loved and respected those people: Lis, his former and current coaches, his former and current team-mates.

What was in his heart? He was not a young man given to deep thought or personal contemplation. But neither was he a mindless young man to whom things just happened. The question of his identity, and how he felt about these matters, wasn't something he would discuss. It wasn't part of his conversation. At that age it wasn't in his conscious thought. But it was somewhere inside him. He was a Murri. He had a strong sense of his Aboriginality – more than people realised, and maybe more than he realised himself. In a way he was being asked to deny that sense of himself in order to fulfil the expectations others had of him. Those expectations were something of a burden. These things boiled away in his subconscious, he now understands, and they concerned him.

Wayne Bennett knew what Steve would have to do. 'Steve had to lose a sense of himself,' he asserts. 'Because [otherwise] he can't make it. If he goes back to his background, to his upbringing, to his Aboriginal heritage, he can't make it. He has to lose himself . . . The things we do are foreign to him. The discipline in training and playing are not part of the Aboriginal culture, particularly when you are strongly Aboriginal. Steve was very Aboriginal. But Elissa has been as much a part of bringing that European part into his life as anyone else.'

The discipline Bennett speaks of is a particular type of discipline, the type required by a football club. The Renoufs had their own form of discipline and commitment, often unspoken. They were committed to each other and they were, and remain, a close family.

Sometimes the sense of discipline valued in football clubs lacks cultural sensitivity. Tony Currie is a Murri himself. In fact, he and

Steve have a lot in common. Both were naturally talented attacking players, both were quick, both had to learn to be defensive players, both were determined to get a trade. (Tony is now a qualified motor mechanic with his own thriving workshop and tyre service.) Although Currie believes that the Broncos have a long way to go to properly understand and respond to Indigenous players, he says they have been better than other clubs. He says that if Steve had gone elsewhere we may never have seen the best of him:

> Fair dinkum, if he'd been recruited to Canterbury straight from Murgon, they would have said, 'Look at this Murri kid from Queensland: he's got no training.' And they would have brushed him. That happens a lot in Sydney. They just assumed that I was a lazy blackfella. I just kept saying 'Give me a go'. I had a stomach problem – six weeks I had some bug. Crook as a dog. One day I nearly fainted at training and Warren Ryan came up to me and said, 'Are you sure you haven't been drinking?'

TC believes a lot of players don't make it because of their cultural background. 'There's a lot of Indigenous guys who go to Sydney. They can all play footy: they've got footwork, speed, hands, they know the game. But they aren't given the opportunity to develop because the hard work and discipline hasn't been in their nature. It has to be grown.'

It certainly grew in Tony Currie. He became a solid, reliable, all-round player who, in developing the type of game required by top footy, never lost his creativity either. He played for Queensland and Australia. TC was good for Steve, and they grew close, in their own way. There was certainly a mutual respect, and that extra something which Indigenous people will tell you that they share.

Currie knew exactly what Steve was going through. He felt

he knew Steve without even meeting him. Currie is a Mullinjali from Beaudesert way. His grandfather grew up on the mission at Fingal in northern New South Wales and played rugby league for NSW Country. He was picked to play against City in 1938, but like many Murris of the time was refused permission to go.

Steve and Tony never broached the subject of their Aboriginality directly. 'Murris don't talk about that stuff,' Tony explains. 'Not formally. A lot is unspoken. But Aboriginal people understand Aboriginal people.'

Currie had seen a lot of young Aboriginal players struggle to come to terms with the requirements of top rugby league. Prospects like Shane Duffy came and went. Clubs explained their departure with phrases like 'went off the rails' or 'gone walkabout'. This was a gross over-simplification of a complex situation, and one which affirmed stereotypical views. Tony and Steve both remember an incident at the Broncos concerning a recruit from west of Toowoomba whose name they don't even remember. TC tells the story:

> Kelvin Giles was belting out his sergeant-major stuff, getting stuck in: run till you bleed through the eyes. That type of stuff. Then this young Murri kid give it to him. 'I'm goin'. I'm goin' home.' Up he got and jumped into his car. We were at Kelvin Grove Teachers' College and we thought he was going home to his flat. But he was going home – back to the bush. We never saw him again. You say things to each other like, 'He should have stuck it out', or there's talk, 'He's weak'. Instead of sitting down and talking it out with him.

Currie was to be an important teacher for Steve. And he was good at it. Steve needed to feel comfortable about becoming a disciplined footballer and that's exactly how Currie made Steve feel. 'TC was a great help,' Steve acknowledges. 'You never felt he thought he was too good for you. He was someone you could go and talk to. And TC loves talking. He always had something good to say to you.' Renowned for his defensive skills, Currie was asked by Bennett to help Steve with that side of his game. Teams like Canberra had targeted Steve, running at him consistently until he was physically and mentally affected. (Try wrapping your 18-year-old chicken arms around the monster thighs of Big Mal.) That had to change.

It was to be a gradual process over a number of seasons. Talk with TC. Watch TC. Work with TC. Practise. Practise. Practise. Talk with TC. Watch TC. Talk with TC. Then it was a matter of confidence. (When Trevor Gillmeister came along, he helped as well.) 'I struggled with my defence,' Steve admits. 'They helped. The big thing with TC was technique. TC always talked about technique. Positioning had been my downfall. If I got a hold of someone, no worries, but I struggled to get myself in the right spot.'

A few good hits in matches and that confidence started to grow. Steve was also maturing physically. It was significant that he was becoming bigger and stronger, but, says Currie, it was more significant that he *believed* he was stronger. He was pressing good weights and had lost that boyish look. Kelvin Giles had them all on solid programs. 'I remember when Kelvin Giles came,' Steve says, 'we were all negative. Who's this bloke, telling us what to do? But he turned the place upside down in strength. After my first session with him my arms seized up. I needed physio the next day to get them straight again! But I started to see the benefits. I put on weight and I felt stronger.'

The Broncos were well-prepared for the 1990 season. The prospects looked good. The club had some new faces. Kevin Walters was lured home from Canberra, a signing which was to have a significant impact on the career of Steve Renouf and the fortunes of the Broncos. Gaven Allen was back from St George to replace Bryan Niebling who had retired after a terrific career, and yet another centre, Dale Shearer, joined from Manly. A couple of promising outside backs were emerging from the junior ranks as well. It was hot competition if you were a three-quarter at the Broncos.

The club was not without its problems. There were tensions between the coach and the captain. Wayne Bennett and Wally Lewis are both very strong personalities and they weren't seeing eye to eye. Bennett was determined to take the side in his direction. His decision to make Gene Miles captain caused a stir from Normanton to Nobby Beach. The reins went to Miles ostensibly to allow Lewis time to carry out his role in the media, but there was probably a bit more to it.

Steve didn't pay much attention to club politics. In some ways the thirty-somethings were a world away from him; in other ways he was their team-mate. He spent more time with the players his own age, although he always got on with Sam Backo. 'Big Sammy,' he says with a smile, 'and that scratchy voice. He'd always say, "Hey brother", and he'd have a big hug for me.' Steve loved the special connection he had with the Aboriginal and Islander players.

With the new season about to kick off, Steve felt pretty good. He wanted a consistent First Grade spot and he felt ready to take it. He'd just have to do more than his competitors when the opportunities came. Bennett gave him a run. He played solidly in the first two pre-season matches but then injured his ankle while scoring the second of his tries against Canterbury in the Nissan Sevens. It was an untimely setback.

After the ankle improved he played a couple of First Grade games. But there were more problems. Late one week, having been selected in First Grade, he had pain in his shin. He didn't say anything. It got worse through training, almost unbearable, so he went off to see the Broncos doctor, Peter Friis, who confirmed his fears: it wasn't just shin soreness, but an actual stress fracture.

A footballer has a difficult relationship with his body. Just as Steve felt close to becoming a regular First Grader, his body let him down. He was extremely disappointed. He was out of football for seven weeks.

During that time two new faces made the most of their chances: Paul Hauff, the tall policeman, managed to tie up the full-back spot, and the boy from Roma, Willie Carne, showed tremendous pace on a wing. It seemed they had come from nowhere and their inclusion demonstrated that Wayne Bennett would reward anyone who performed, rather than bowing to reputation. His youth policy was paying dividends.

Steve didn't begrudge his team-mates their chance. He knew full well that a club is stronger when players are competing for spots in the top side. He just set about working his way back through Reserve Grade, coached that season by Billy Gardiner. The form of Hauff and Carne never tapered, and they were named joint rookies of the year.

Steve was given the occasional opportunity in First Grade. Having played his Reserve Grade game, he was often asked to sit on the First Grade bench. It frustrated him terribly. One day he was picked as a specialist reserve and didn't get a run at all. For Steve this was the pits. He wanted to play football, even if it was in a lower grade, not sit and watch it. Bennett knew that, and that week he sought Steve out to explain why he hadn't used him. It had been a tight encounter and he didn't want to take his experienced players off.

Steve played just four First Grade games. But it was also a valuable season, because he was working on his defensive skills and his positional play – and, as always, he was scoring plenty of tries. Fifteen in all. His match-altering brilliance hadn't deserted him. He led the Reserve Grade into the Grand Final with tries in each of the semifinals.

Midway through the finals series Steve's grandmother died. Nan South was 90, and had been a magnificent character. Steve was deeply saddened, as was the whole family. They celebrated her remarkable life, and grieved her passing. The family had always derived great strength from her resilience and from the love she had for her people. They told the stories of how Cherbourg was always her team. When Steve played for Wondai against Cherbourg she would say, 'I can't cheer for you fellas, but when no one's looking I do.' She stood before the world without apology, confident in her sense of self, a proud and dignified Aboriginal person.

Steve tried to get his mind on football. The Broncos were out of the First Grade race, but it seemed much of Queensland was behind the Reserve Grade side. The team included quite a few country lads and Steve got on well with them. There was a good feeling among them. The skipper, Ray Herring, was from Oakey on the Darling Downs. He knew Steve was a class above them in Reserve Grade. He also knew the value of formulating a strong sense of team identity, at any level of football, over a season. Reserve Grade teams can be teams in their own right, not just stepping stones to the top level. Ray Herring's team was deter-mined to win the Broncos' first main-season trophy.

Steve had an outstanding grand final. He made numerous breaks. He had a try disallowed when it looked like he'd snuck over from, of all places, dummy half. The tight match finished 6–6. They went to extra time. Tired bodies lifted, but Canberra looked to be getting on top. They made a break. Steve found himself the sole defender 10 metres out with three Raiders coming at him. It was all over. They were gone. He waited until the last instant, when, just as his opponent was drawing him to pass outside, he faked to tackle and knocked the pass down. Soon after, Herring struck at a lazy play-the-ball and toed the football through. It ricocheted off the upright, lobbed in his lap and the battered skipper fell over the line.

Still, Canberra wouldn't lie down, and it looked like they would tie the match up when Bell strode into the clear. Again all he had to do was beat Renouf. Pearl stood there and pummelled him in a strong, front-on, last-ditch tackle. Twice Steve Renouf's *defence* had saved the day.

Victory to the Broncos. Cheers throughout Queensland. Steve Renouf: Man of the Match. In accepting the award, he looked down the barrel of the television camera and said in his Pearl way, 'Thanks to the State Bank and g'day to everyone back home in Murgon.'

Murgon people have never forgotten that.

CHAPTER 7

Success

JOHN RIBOT HAD watched Steve Renouf's Man-of-the-Match performance with much interest. He knew Steve stood out and that he would have caught the eye of some astute judges. He could imagine the conversations among club officials on the prowl: 'That Aboriginal centre goes alright.'

Steve Renouf drew attention to himself by the grace of his movement that day. But it wasn't just that. It was the way he influenced the Grand Final, the way he handled the pressure, the way things happened when he was near the football. Ribot knew the kid would be an asset to any club. He'd bring people through the gate. He'd win matches for his club.

As Steve was about to get on the team bus later that afternoon he was surprised to hear John Ribot calling after him. 'Bucko,' Ribot said. 'I'll talk to you next week. We need to get a new contract signed.' Steve hadn't given any of that sort of stuff a thought. He was just happy to have won another premiership.

In those days, Steve looked after his own affairs. He was not one for false modesty. He had some idea of what he could do with a football in his hands. But he still wasn't confident enough to think he was going to be a regular First Grader. After all, he'd just spent a season in Reserve Grade. He had only a vague idea of what he was worth to a football club. And he wasn't one to ask for things.

He signed a modest contract for three years, which included the standard Broncos bonus for playing in winning sides. He and Lis were happy with that.

The Brisbane Broncos club has always been a sporting business, and, as much as we watch footy without thinking about that commercial imperative, it is always there. The club's administrators have always known the tension between sentiment and sound business practice.

That culture was illustrated perfectly by the decision to let Wally Lewis go after the 1990 season. Fans could hardly believe it. Here was a young club releasing one of the greatest players the world of rugby league had ever seen. Wayne Bennett argued that if the club continued to pay Lewis what he was worth and still remain within the salary cap it would have to offer the younger players, like Steve, very little. This would make them easy targets for Sydney clubs.

Steve had already signed. He just wanted to get the summer fitness slog out of the way, and on with the 1991 season. And it was a slog. But when the pre-season matches got under way, he fired. He quickly found form. 'Renouf set for a spot in the back-line' and 'Hopefuls stake claims' read the *Courier-Mail* headlines. Bennett was impressed. After Steve scored two tries and played a hand in another two against North Sydney in Bundaberg, the coach said, 'We have always known the kid had ability, it was just a matter of finding spaces for everyone . . . Steve will put a lot of pressure on everyone in the three-quarters now he knows he is right at home in this standard.'

Steve was patient. 'All I can do is play well and hope for

the best,' he told *Rugby League Week*. He was also respectful of the centres – Miles, Shearer, Johns, Jackson and Currie. 'Getting into First Grade at the Broncos is as tough a thing as there is to achieve in rugby league.'

After two more solid performances, Bennett announced, 'It has taken Steve three years in his development, but I have no doubt he is well and truly ready for First Grade.' So he picked him in the centres for the opening fixture.

Steve always felt encouraged when people showed confidence in him. He didn't let Bennett down in the match against Manly. 'Renouf was the most dangerous runner on the field,' the *Sydney Morning Herald* reported. 'He was everywhere and crossed for an intercept try in the Broncos 12–2 victory.'

People were seeing what Steve could do. He was the subject of numerous media profiles. David Fordham interviewed him at the Yeronga TAFE for Channel 7. In a moment of true art, a shot of Steve wiring up a circuit board was accompanied by Fordo's voiceover, 'Steve Renouf has provided the spark for the Broncos backline.'

The *Courier-Mail* produced a substantial personal history of Steve which included an interview with his father and numerous family photos of the Renoufs during Steve's childhood. Old Charlie loved it. The piece also included a photo of Steve with Lis. Thus began the ongoing and significant portrayal of Steve as a loyal, family-orientated young man.

Steve's good form continued. He looked brilliant with the football, but his defence was still a talking point. In the Round 3 clash against Canberra he had to mark Mal Meninga. It was a tough way to get to know the big man, especially since he was Steve's childhood hero. 'I was a bit nervous at the start,' he told *Courier-Mail* sports writer Crash Craddock, 'but you can't afford to worry about one particular player. Mal was one of my idols as a kid. I remember watching him on the ABC's *Big League* . . . He is bloody hard to tackle . . . The second time he fended me off today I didn't know where I was. I saw stars. But you just have to come back.' Steve kept at it, and played his part in the Broncos win. Meninga was more than a little impressed, hinting that Renouf might partner him in the centres in the first State of Origin match. 'He is a good open field runner,' the big Queenslander said, 'and will improve with experience. He is playing well in the Sydney competition so I think he would handle the next level of play up.'

It was all unfolding so quickly. Steve was becoming the player others thought he could be. On ABC TV newsreader Rod Young introduced a segment with the words: 'Steve Renouf has been hailed as one of the brightest talents in rugby league for years – not least by his own coach.' An interview with Bennett followed. 'That's the great thing about the champions,' the coach said, 'they've all got their own characteristics – and he's in that cate-gory. Steve was reasonably lazy and had a lot of skill but he has learnt what the Broncos' expectations are and fitted in accord-ingly.' Steve was then interviewed and typically deflected all praise.

Back in Murgon the Renouf family always gathered around the TV to watch Bucko play, whoever was at home: Mum and Dad, sisters and brothers, nephews and nieces, friends. Charlie just loved that Steve was getting on top of things; that he was making his way in rugby league. He couldn't have been prouder.

When the *Courier-Mail*'s Paul Malone picked his possible State of Origin side he included Steve in the centres because Queensland desperately needed pace and attacking firepower. The selectors were of a similar mind, naming Steve on the wing.

At just 20 – easily the youngest player in the side – Steve was playing at what was regarded by many as the highest level. State of Origin football was certainly the most intense. Some were describing his inclusion as a meteoric rise, paying attention only to the previous couple of months. It had, of course, been three years in the making, a process of advance and setback; a process during which Steve had really been tested. So being selected meant a lot to him, especially as he would be playing alongside Mal Meninga.

The famous State of Origin camps had a mystique about them. They were like meetings of some secret society; gatherings of the finest rugby league players in the world. There was no initiation, but as Steve settled into the Travelodge in Roma Street just down from Lang Park, he felt he'd become part of an inner sanctum.

He had heard the stories about Origin week from some of his Broncos team-mates: about the solid training, the plotting to beat the Blues, and the build-up to the series. It didn't take him long to realise that interstate football was absolutely fair dinkum. Even the most experienced players were excited and nervous about it all.

There were ways to relieve the tension. Whenever the squad had to go somewhere they went in Wally's Bus. Lewis drove the legendary vehicle in his own way. It was a beast of a thing and often had the better of The King, who bunny-hopped it around the place. He'd gun it down Cochrane Street in Red Hill and they'd be airborne over the speed bumps. Wally would turn around and say 'Don't worry, boys' and he'd be giving a running commentary of the punters in the street. 'Look at this bloke,' he'd say. 'Poor ol' bugger's a bit thirsty. Hasn't had a beer since brekkie.'

He was like Randall P. MacMurphy from *One Flew Over the Cuckoo's Nest* driving the boys around for the day. Sometimes they'd adjust the windscreen squirters, turning them to point outwards, then drive along Latrobe Terrace spraying the pedestrians. People would get a fright and they'd quickly look up: 'What was that?' Then they'd realise: 'Just the Queensland State of Origin team.'

A few beers helped as well, and Steve heard plenty of yarns about the great days of old: stories like 'How Jacko got his nickname' and 'Jacko and the nude squat sessions'. It was often Jacko. He was called Mylanta Mouth, a sobriquet conferred on him by the senior players because he was always on the Mylanta tablets at training if he was coming off a big night. Trying to train and chew, he looked like he was frothing at the mouth.

The camp also gave Steve a chance to get to know Mal Meninga. Other than wearing his massive thigh on his shoulder and his palm in his face a few times, Steve had had little contact with Mal. He made no secret of his respect for the giant centre, and that he had been an inspiration to him as a boy. Mal talked and Steve listened.

Steve enjoyed the company but he was also feeling the pressure. He had a pretty good idea of what he was in for.

A State of Origin game played in Brisbane at Lang Park is one of the sporting highlights of the Queensland year. It has become deeply entrenched in the life of the state. Queenslanders who are not lucky enough to be at the ground are at parties or barbecues or at pubs pumped and ready for a big game.

The matches are battles of attrition between two warring lines. They are frenzied confrontations where bodies clash at full pace, and where that little extra in the exchanges is excused on the grounds that 'it's State of Origin'.

This game was no exception. Steve sat on the bench. The two packs belted into each other. Mark Geyer, no angel, threw himself around giving away penalties. For much of the game the Maroons led 2–0. There seemed to be no let-up in the physical intensity. And hardly a break in play. Queensland lounge rooms were ready to explode.

Paul Hauff had a blinder until midway through the second half when he dislocated his shoulder. Steve went on. Shortly after, Meninga hit a pass 10 metres out and no one could stop him. Over. Queensland: 6–0 with the kick to come. To an ad break at last. And if Queenslanders weren't feeling Maroon enough, it was that Fourex ad with the boys at the beach:

Fish are jumpin', waves are pumpin',
Steak is sizzlin', this is livin',
An ocean as blue as the sky up above us
We love it up here.
We don't just like it, we love it:
The people, the places,
The mates, the faces,
The XXXX mate,
We love it up here.

Mal missed the kick. Laurie Daley scored and it was 6–4. Michael O'Connor had a chance to tie it up with the conversion from the sideline. He missed. Relief. Then, just as the game seemed secure, Mal's kick-off sailed over the dead-ball line. Penalty. So all of Queensland watched as Greg Alexander took the shot from the halfway line, after the siren, to level the scores. The kick fell short.

It was a grinding win for the Maroons. Queensland coach, Graham Lowe, was chaired off by Marty Bella and a battle-scarred Wally Lewis whose eye was cut, swollen and quickly closing. Steve had played his small part, making a couple of tackles. It had been a wild old game of footy.

While Steve had been in good touch before that first Origin match, a few indifferent weeks followed. His patchy form coincided with a string of Bronco losses, a perennial problem during the Origin weeks. In one match he and Kevvy Walters were defending side by side. Only they weren't defending. They gave the green light to a few Canterbury attackers and hardly laid a hand on them. 'They just ran through us at will,' Kevvy recalls. 'I blamed Pearl. Pearl blamed me. The coach blamed both of us.'

Steve wasn't picked for the other Origin matches. Queensland lost the second encounter but went on to win the decider 14–12. It was Wally Lewis's last Origin contest.

Steve settled into the rhythm of the home-and-away season. He had cemented his position and had the crowds cheering. His instinct remained dominant: he was still very much an attacking player. He had to force himself to be conscious of defence and to think about winning matches. In fact he often had to be reminded to think in terms of defence. But he was coming to terms with the idea of being a Bronco, of subjugating himself to the demands of the football club.

Sometimes he was naive about situations. After a good win at Marathon Stadium, the Broncos were guests at a function at a Newcastle hotel. Steve was enjoying a Crown Lager when Bernie Power, the owner of Power's Brewery, one of the Broncos' major sponsors, walked past. 'Would you like a drink, Steve?' he asked. Steve thought it was kind of him to offer but gestured with his Crownie and said, 'No thanks, mate.' Bernie, through gritted teeth, retorted, 'No, Steve, would you like a beer?' The penny dropped: he wasn't drinking the sponsor's product.

Steve was certainly becoming more comfortable at the Broncos, but if he was going to feel at home there he would have to find genuine substitutes for what he'd left behind in Murgon: his family, and a place where he felt he belonged. Lis and Wayne Bennett and his team-mates provided a sense of family; Fulcher Road, Lang Park and to an extent the city of Brisbane were becoming important places for him.

It was a different feeling, though, and in some ways Steve's sense of himself as an Aboriginal person was being moved, even pushed, to the side. Much of that sense of Aboriginality came through his family and he was away from them. He was also, understandably, preoccupied with football.

He was playing for a club that was perceived as a very good sporting organisation. There was a strong football culture and a strong commercial culture. These were the parameters by which most people in the community measured the Broncos.

But there are other measures. And the Broncos was not a club that celebrated cultural difference. Certainly, players were free to be whoever they wanted to be – there was no doubt about that – but only as long as it did not encroach upon their performance at the Broncos. When you were at the Broncos, you were a Bronco. According to Broncos psychologist Phil Jauncey, the Broncos concentrate on the moment. 'What you did before you came to the Broncos doesn't matter. It's what you do now that matters. And you're expected to be a Bronco. When you're here, you're family.'

The club may have been a family but it was one in which acceptance as a family member was conditional on behaving in certain ways. In his own family, Steve had known unconditional acceptance. 'At the Broncos,' says Jauncey, 'you either fit in or you go somewhere else. What's relevant is what you can do here. At the Broncos it is not about denying self, it's that self is not a relevant [concept]. At the Broncos you're not a Catholic, you're not a Greek, you're not a vegetarian, you're not smart or thick, you're not an Aboriginal. You're a Bronco.'

Wayne Bennett wasn't exactly Don Corleone but there were times when it felt like he was: a godfather figure who wanted the best for his boys, but on his terms. If players chose football and the Broncos, they made that choice knowing what the expectations were. They had to trust Bennett. They had to believe he had their best interests at heart.

Bennett acknowledges that he didn't always get it right. In those early days he was quite intense and strong-willed about how things would happen. But Steve did trust Bennett, and the further they went the better they got to know each other. Bennett believed there were big things ahead for Steve Renouf. That faith gave Steve a real lift.

For a young player, Steve had an impressive season. But, overall, the Broncos 1991 performances were not consistent enough. It wasn't until August that they gathered momentum, winning their last five matches, only to miss out on the finals by a single game. Penrith won the Winfield Cup in a year that had seen the Broncos beat each of the top five sides. To figure in the finals they needed to find a way around the pressures of the representative season.

Missing out on the final five meant that Steve and Lis were able to get back to Murgon. Paul Bishop had pulled the boots on for the Murgon Mustangs for many years and he was playing his last game. Steve and Lis were glad to be there to see the match and celebrate with him. A couple of weeks later Steve was the special guest at the Murgon football club's end-of-year function, where he presented the trophies and awards (including one to Bish for best club player in the finals). His short speech was reported in the *South Burnett Times*: 'It is very satisfying to come home and to see the success of the friends I played with in under-age teams. It shows the character of this place. These guys have done much better than we [the Broncos] did and I'd like to pay tribute to them for that.'

It was an emotional night. Murgon-Goomeri had won the A Grade premiership under their much-loved skipper Frankie Malone, who had finally decided to retire after fourteen years in A Grade. He shared the honour of best club player for the season with forward Bill Adcock. It was a memorable moment for

Frankie when he and Steve stood together centre stage and he received his award.

The night meant a lot to Steve as well.

During the 1992 pre-season, Steve received the devastating news that his father had suffered a massive heart attack and died. While Charlie hadn't been in the greatest of health, no one had expected something like this. He was 63.

Steve and Lis headed straight back to Murgon. Steve loved his father. He loved his father's quiet encouragement. He loved how his father taught him to be happy, to feel free, to understand that some things were beyond your control, that other things you could have a crack at, that you could fight against the things which needed fighting against. And to enjoy life when it was good. Really enjoy it. He loved how his dad got so much from his children's happiness; how he loved a laugh.

Charlie's love of life had been an inspiration to many in the community. He had played a vital role in establishing two important organisations: the legal service and the housing service. But for the Renouf family he was not only an inspiration but a husband and a father and his death left a long emptiness.

The funeral was held at the Salvation Army church in Murgon. A huge congregation attended: his extended family, many from the Aboriginal community, many townsfolk, and many who would never forget the colourful character. Steve was a pall-bearer.

As he came out of the church carrying the weight of his father's body, he saw the crowd before him. Wayne Bennett and Glenn Lazarus were there, along with other football friends, as were John McHugh and John Hunter from the Mater Hospital, and people like Matt Foley who'd worked with Charlie. He was at once saddened to the core of his being and uplifted by the response of these people.

The months that followed were difficult. Steve spent a lot of time with his family, and with Lis. But for all the sadness it was also a happy and hopeful time. Not long after Charlie passed on, Lis found out that she was pregnant, the timing making the news all the more poignant.

Life went on. Steve continued his apprenticeship at the Mater even though he was now able to make a reasonable living from football. He still wanted to get his trade, and he enjoyed working there.

Wayne Bennett had recruited Lazarus from Canberra that summer. His work up front was to be invaluable throughout his career in Brisbane. He was experienced, level-headed and very, very strong and would have the pack going forward. The backs were rubbing their hands together.

There are no guarantees for the prospects of any season. But the Broncos had a lot of talented players who were getting to the age where they were still in great shape physically and had the experience of around one hundred games behind them – Alfie Langer, Kevin and Kerrod Walters, Mick Hancock, Chris Johns, Terry Matterson among others. Steve was a little younger, but he was fast becoming one of the finest centres in the league.

The Broncos looked impressive in the pre-season games, stringing together a series of wins, although they lost the final of the competition to Illawarra. The premiership season also started well. There was a good feeling in the squad and a sense that they were enjoying their football. They were scoring some sensational tries from all over the park.

Steve was more relaxed around the club. He still didn't say much but he laughed a lot. There were some real characters pulling on the Broncos jumper in those days. Alfie was the best half-back in the world, but that didn't stop him from being afraid of the dark. He and Kevvy roomed together and Kevvy reckons that Alf always made him take the bed near the window so the burg-u-lars would get him first. They were always having a go at each other.

The coach also mellowed. Steve reckons that Wayne Bennett changed a lot during those early years at the Broncos, partly because he came to realise that it was going to be near impossible to change blokes like Kevvy and Alf. He learnt that it was going to be more productive to work with them, rather than to be constantly fighting their natures. 'Wayne was tough at the start,' Steve says. 'He was intense. And I think he had to learn to loosen up because he had these players around who were jokers. That's why he is so good. Because he realised a certain style wouldn't work with players like Alf and Kevvy. *He* learnt to fit in. He realised he couldn't go against the grain of the team.'

A happy chemistry was developing. The side racked up win after win. The weeks passed in a pleasant routine. They would have a win on the weekend and celebrate it. Then they'd get together for Monday Club where they had a steak and a few beers and took it easy. Each player got his win bonus – an envelope with $792 in it. In those days the players were paid half their contract money in July and half in October, and often they'd find themselves short. So Monday Club kept them going.

It was a casual and relaxed night, but an important night, as Kevvy explains: 'It was a way of everyone squaring off with each other. We'd get our pays and fix whoever up. Mostly Alf. We used to call him the ATM. He was always the one with all the cash on him. If you needed fifty you'd go and steal it off Alf. "Pay you back Monday, Alf." It made Alf play well – to get us over the line so he'd get his money back. That's what made him the player that he was.'

The Broncos won twenty-two games that year, losing only four. Steve could feel a healthy confidence growing. He could feel the respect for each other, the belief in each other. They were convinced they could win any game they played in.

They didn't have the most structured attack in rugby league. In fact Steve can't remember any of the moves or their names, except for one – the simple move which became their trademark. 'We didn't like too much structure,' he admits. 'We just used to ad lib it. That was the beauty of our team. Nothing too complex.'

That free-running approach brought dividends. They became known for attacking from broken play and for throwing the ball around well inside their own territory. While other sides bashed it up with their big forwards and made 40 metres in five tackles, the Broncos would swing it wide and make 60 metres in three tackles, and then be well and truly on the attack. Often it was Pearl who'd make the break. But he didn't have much of a second effort. 'We'd attack from inside our own half all the time. So I'd be running my ring off,' he says. 'Often we wouldn't score and they'd be looking for you again. I'd shake my head. And I'd have a spell.'

At times Steve would actively avoid the action. Everyone knew what he could do, but unless he felt right and ready he wouldn't do it. It used to drive Kevvy nuts. Here was the most creative centre in the world and he didn't want the pill.

'Steve didn't get involved much and he didn't say much,' Kevvy reckons. 'He'd rather just sit out there and not get the ball. But Alf and I used to make him run.'

Alf was like a cranky mother: 'Pearl, get out there. And I'm going to pass it to you.' Or Kevvy would look over to catch his attention to set up the next play and Steve would cover his near eye with his cupped hand and, like a schoolboy avoiding the teacher, pretend he didn't see. Then Kevvy would catch Steve's eye again and say, 'Pearl, next tackle it's comin' to you.' And, according to Walters, he'd say, 'No. No. Next one. Next one.' 'But sure enough,' says Kevvy, 'he'd be ready.'

Alfie, Kevvy and Steve developed one of the most successful combinations in rugby league. Yet they had only one formal move which they worked time and time again; a basic move which, despite looking ridiculously simple, took opposition defences years to work out. Only in recent times have attacks been able to mimic it. It was their 'go-to' play, and Steve was their 'go-to' man. It was called the 'outball', a term which has now become part of rugby league vocabulary.

Steve remembers when it first happened. They didn't so much invent it as discover it. After Kevvy had thrown a pass and Steve had made a break, they thought, 'That worked.' So that week they looked at the tapes and tried to work out what had happened. And did it again. And again.

The successfully executed outball play provided one of those rare transcendent moments that can happen in sport. It seemed to have some quality, like a wave at Burleigh; a power that is hard to identify but you just know is there. You feel you are watching something pure.

It looked so innocuous and in some ways it was. In other ways its success depended on the exquisite skills of two very capable men. Kevvy Walters had to choose the right moment to call it. He then had to get into the right position and throw the right pass. But it was up to Pearl to make the pass work, and his brilliance allowed him to do that.

Kevvy explains: 'We were just trying to get the ball on the outside of the defender. The ball would just sit there and with his speed Pearl would get there.'

Steve's explanation is similar: 'Kevvy would be floating across and I'd hold, hold, hold. It was about keeping that opposing centre sucked in [towards the ruck] for as long as possible and then, BANG, you're gone. He'd put it across the face of that defender.'

It wasn't too complicated. So why did it work? 'What we really relied on,' Steve says, 'was that their centre was never looking at the ball, they were always looking at me. And nine times out of ten they were. So the guy's looking at me, and next thing the ball's beaten him and I've just got to get myself there to where the ball is.'

As always, Steve underestimates his own role in it all. His spooky anticipation, remarkable timing, scintillating acceleration and amazing balance were all significant factors. He would just slice through the line and be away. Once he had some room, his pace and evasive skills would take him further down the park and often over the line. He scored many times without anyone putting a hand on him in circumstances where everyone – team-mates, opponents, commentators and fans – wondered what had happened. Defenders couldn't work out what was going on.

'He used to suck his arse in a little bit too; that skinny arse of his.' Kevvy laughs as he remembers. 'He didn't need a fend. It was just a swipe. But they weren't grabbing anything. He was just too quick. They'd go to tackle him and just get nothing. It wasn't until a few years later when they worked out what he was doing that he developed that fend. Early on they weren't getting near him.'

One of Andrew Johns' first games was against Brisbane (in 1994). He found himself defending the right side of the field. 'I was just blown away by the pace on him,' Johns admits. 'But also the lines he used to run. He and Kevvy had that outball game. One minute you'd be marked up on him. You'd take your eyes off him, next minute he's 10 metres away. He was so quick off the mark and so well-balanced. I was never quick enough to be close enough to get the fend.'

Johns eventually learnt to throw a similar outball. Darren Lockyer is good enough to throw it, and remarkably he can play the Renouf role as well. If it's being thrown for him he knows where to be to best receive it. A lot of that he learnt from Pearl and Kevvy.

'It was something other teams wanted to do,' Steve says. 'And we'd go into Australian camps and they'd try and get it out of us. And Kevvy would say, "Pearl, don't you go tellin' 'em" – because I was a bit younger and a bit naive. But Kevvy wasn't giving any Broncos' secrets away. So I used to say, "I don't know. We just do it. It just happens."'

Steve worked with Alf and Chris Johns as well as Kevvy. He'd run off the forwards if one got through and he could be bothered getting there in support. He loved a try, so he was often backing up, and once he got the football he'd set sail. Mick Hancock reckons that if Steve hadn't been such a good finisher he'd have scored a lot more tries himself. Often Steve had no need to give the ball to him.

That year New South Wales won the third State of Origin match to take the series 2–1. When a couple of the Queensland regulars were unavailable because of injury, Steve was picked on the bench for the first match, the only one he played in that series. He was happy to concentrate on helping chalk up wins for the Broncos.

Hitting top form towards the end of the home-and-away season, the Broncos won eleven of their last twelve matches to finish top and, under the final five system, win the valued week off. They came into the play-offs as the team to beat.

It was a memorable September. Wayne Bennett was always very strong on the idea that his players should really enjoy the finals month. He wanted his teams to savour the time. It was one of Bennett's many strengths, that he helped the players deal with the sense of apprehension which often accompanies high expectations. Finals were like life: not to be encountered fearfully but to be celebrated. By virtue of your week in, week out home-and-away performance, you had won the opportunity to show the world what you could do. And you had every right to take that opportunity. Which is why finals meant so much to Steve, and he looks back on them so fondly. It wasn't about what they couldn't do, it was about what they could do.

Somehow Bennett had released much of the tension. Steve felt relaxed. He even had a chance to spend time with the Year 4 and 5 students from Cherbourg State School who were on a school excursion to Brisbane to see the Broncos train. Of course Steve was their favourite and he spoke to them about how they could achieve what they hoped to achieve.

The Broncos trained well in that first week. There were meetings and discussions. On the Saturday night the whole Broncos outfit – players, wives and girlfriends, managers and strappers – went to an Italian restaurant in Caxton Street. They took it easy as their opponents slogged it out in the finals in Sydney. It was a classic night. A big night – even by Broncos standards. Wayne Bennett and his wife Trish were relaxed and enjoying themselves. Spirits were high. And then they had another week to prepare for the semifinal against Illawarra.

The break was invaluable. Steve loved feeling fresh. He was the sort of player who, if he felt especially good before a game, would perform well. The semifinal against Illawarra was billed as the clash of the centres: Steve and Chris Johns up against Brett Rodwell and Paul McGregor. During the week Channel 7 reporter Patty Welsh had interviewed Steve and hinted it would be a big task to contain the robust Steelers' pair. Steve seemed unperturbed, if not quietly confident, suggesting that the crowd might be a factor, that the Broncos would 'get off on the crowd being against us'.

The Broncos started the major semifinal slowly. But they started to spin the footy out wide whenever they could, Kevvy and Steve working their typical combinations. Trailing 6–0 they took the risk of running the ball on the sixth tackle and Pearl got away. He was nailed deep in Steelers' territory. A couple of minutes later Kevvy scored. From there the Broncos took over. They won 22–12. Alf scored twice.

Steve had a superb game. Illawarra coach Graham Murray was left scratching his head. He described him as 'unstoppable'. 'If you go low on Renouf he gets the pass away. If you go high he palms you off,' he lamented.

Walters knew exactly where the game had been won. 'We more or less got them out in the centres,' he told Steve Ricketts in the *Courier-Mail*. 'Steve's strong running in the first half really lifted us after that tough opening 20 minutes.'

The Broncos win took them straight into the Grand Final, and gave them another week off. Brisbane, indeed Queensland, was abuzz. A lot of the talk was of Renouf. Fans knew their team was in with a big chance, whoever the Broncos played, and Steve had a lot to do with that. If Test cricket is about having a strike bowler who can take wickets, like Dennis Lillee, rugby league is about having a player who can pierce the line. Steve had something which made him one of the few players who could do that consistently. His semifinal performance had again brought him to the attention of the Australian selectors, as well as the media and the public. There was even interest in him in Sydney.

People wanted to know more about him. A photo of Steve and Lis appeared in the Sydney *Daily Telegraph*. The accompanying article told of the expected birth of their first child six weeks after the Grand Final. Lis was quoted as saying that she had virtually no interest in football! 'I'll have to be honest,' she admitted, 'I'm always watching Steve more than the match.'

The Ipswich Connection wasn't going to let Steve have all the limelight. In inimitable fashion the clown princes, Alf, Kevvy and Kerrod, released a single, 'Hey Hey We're the Broncos', with Monkee-esque lines like:

Hey, hey we're the Broncos
And we're not horsin' around
We're too busy training
Trying to lift the Winfield Crown

Interviewed by Billy J. Smith for Channel 10, Kerrod Walters played the serious rock idol. 'The fan mail's been comin' in,' he said, poker-faced. '[Being a rock star] is something we've had to deal with over the last few weeks.' But when he tried to say, 'We might put an album down soon,' it was too much and he and Billy J. just cracked up. It was typical of the sense of fun that enveloped the club at that time.

There was another team dinner on the Saturday night of preliminary final week. Again it was a huge night, not unlike the first one. Steve reckons those two dinners were some of the best functions he's been part of.

Going into Grand Final week the team was expectant and revelling in the challenge. So was most of Queensland. At that time there was still a sporting cringe in the Sunshine State. There had been no win in the Sheffield Shield. The Brisbane Bears were struggling. And the State of Origin ledger was pretty evenly balanced. Queenslanders yearned for sporting success as if it were some sort of personal measure. They charged the Broncos with the responsibility to prove that the Maroon type, the punter living in the north, was okay; that the sunshine and the sand and the Bundy, the prawn sandwiches and the boiled peanuts, hadn't softened their heads. The 1992 NSW Rugby League Grand Final mattered to them. They wanted Arko pacing up and down in his

Philip Street office like The Penguin in *Batman,* wondering what he'd done wrong and planning his revenge.

It was hard for the young players not to get caught up in that type of emotion, but to a degree it was good they did. They felt alive. Crowds turned out to training. There were journalists and TV cameras everywhere.

The situation was new to the coach as well. But amid the excitement Wayne Bennett was able to keep things calm and controlled, and to nurture the prevalent belief the team was ready. The key was that no team member doubted that.

On Grand Final day, the Sydney Football Stadium was a mass of red and white. St George fans, St George flags, St George everything. There were pockets of Broncos fans, the most notice-able group having gathered in Bay 39.

Steve wasn't a player who felt nervous before matches. While Alf was fighting to keep his stomach where it was meant to be, Pearl was usually sitting there preparing himself quietly, in his laid-back way. The best preparation for him was not to think too much. Not to anticipate the game, not to play the game before he got out on the track. But on this day there were things on his mind. His mum was up in the stand – but his dad wasn't. Charlie would have loved it. And there was the expectation that Steve would be a key factor in the match. If he played like he had against Illawarra, the Broncos would be hard to hold out.

As the voices filled the dressing room, the enormity of the moment was engulfing Steve. It had become more than a game of football. 'I really felt it,' he remembers. 'I was thinking, "I can't believe we're doing this. I used to watch this on TV at home in Murgon".' He remembers the adrenalin pumping, and feeling drained even before they'd hit the tunnel. 'I probably thought too much,' he says.

On the ground he felt he couldn't get into the game. Not

that they noticed at the Royal Hotel in Murgon where a huge crowd had gathered: family, friends, the Murgon Mustangs crowd, Cherbourg people. Frankie Malone was there. So was Steve's sister Sonia. She was very excited. 'That's just Bucko running around in the NRL Grand Final,' she remembers thinking. It was all rather surreal for her: her ordinary brother doing something extraordinary.

Although they were thrilled in Murgon, Steve felt he was having no influence at all. The Broncos always looked in control of the urgent match without ever building a comfortable lead. The pressure didn't let up. Towards the end of the second half Steve was feeling good for the team but disappointed in his own game. He hadn't played. He hadn't performed. He hadn't shown the world what was in him, what he could do. Then suddenly an opportunity came.

St George were pressing, right on the Broncos line. Willie Carne fielded a chip through and just made it out of the dead-ball area. It had been a frenzied passage of play, and, with players scrambling to get back into position, Kevvy spotted that there was something on straightaway on the left.

'Kevvy initiated it,' Steve remembers. 'He's run into dummy half. He gives it to Alf who threw the pass. I remember stepping Rex Terp and then I knew I was in the clear.' Steve put the foot down. His first thought was that he had a chance to do something at last. He motored away with Ricky Walford chasing. 'As I got going,' he recalls, 'I just thought "Take me, legs" because I just didn't want to get caught. That's all I had in my mind. Just go.'

Meanwhile, in the grandstand the excitement consumed Mrs Renouf. She screamed for her son. She called him on. He crossed the halfway line. He was doing just enough to keep clear of Walford. 'It took a long time,' he recalls. 'I knew Ricky was coming.

And Micky [Hancock] would have been shouting at me on the inside. Mick Potter was gone. He was out of position. I just said, "I've got to get there".'

Over the 20. The 10. Walford dived just as Steve dived, and they fell over the line together. Mrs Renouf was as thrilled as she had ever been in her life. 'There was a white fella standing behind me,' she says, laughing as she remembers. 'I just grabbed him and put my arms around him. I didn't know him from a bar of soap. I bet he got a fright.'

It was a mighty occasion for Steve's mum. Tears filled her happy-sad eyes. 'I just missed old Charlie,' she says. Bruce and Jenny Bishop shed a few tears as well. 'I had them crying too,' Nerida says, chuckling.

Back in Murgon the roof was almost lifted off the Royal Hotel. The crowd erupted as one and cheered Bucko all the way. Beers were sprayed. Blokes who wouldn't move from the stool for an earthquake were on their feet.

It was an unforgettable moment in Australian sport. Two fine Aboriginal players flat out, both moving fluently, Steve just getting there. It has been replayed and replayed. That run, that try, is a key moment not just in Steve Renouf's football career but in his life.

The Broncos won the premiership. It was as joyous an occasion as Steve had ever known. 'It was real jubilation,' he says, remembering the feeling. 'And we felt proud, so proud. We were a close unit and it meant a lot to us.'

The celebrations began. The beers flowed as they flew back to Brisbane. A seat was reserved for the Winfield Cup. When they landed, it seemed the city was ready to party. 'We got off the plane,' Steve remembers, 'but we had no idea of what would be waiting for us. We knew there'd be people there. But it was unbelievable. Indescribable. We're walking down the tunnel and the boys are all whispering to each other, "What about the noise?"'

The players were genuinely surprised and genuinely uplifted by the enormous crowd that had gathered. It made them realise what football meant to these people, people who had invested their hopes in their much-loved footy side over a whole year, people who were so happy and grateful that their boys had won the day.

'We walked out,' Steve remembers, 'and it was just huge. We were walking through and you could tell we were all thinking, "How good's this?"' Alf had that sheepish look on his face, as if he couldn't believe this was all happening to a little bloke from Ipswich. Fans were screaming. Recognising players. Waving flags. Reaching out. Clapping. Yahooing. Cheering. There were tears. 'We were so proud,' Steve remembers.

Somehow they made it onto the bus, but the crowd didn't thin. Cars lined Airport Drive and the people waved and tooted. Then on to King George Square in the heart of Brisbane, which was jam-packed with happy people in carnival mood.

And still further: home to Fulcher Road which was a seething mass of bodies. On getting out of the bus the boys were crowd-surfed by the fans all the way across the ground and over to the clubhouse, where the festivities continued.

What is joy? Is it working together in some common purpose? Is it overcoming obstacles? Is it remembering for a moment what you've done to achieve what you set out to achieve? Is it thinking about your father, and wishing he were standing next to you? Is it thinking about all those who have helped you arrive at this moment?

For Steve it wasn't just about him, it was about those around him. The people he'd sat with over the years. Lis, her tummy bulging with their child. His family. His friends. His team-mates. Wayne Bennett. All just thrilled.

The team celebrated all night at the clubhouse. Then after breakfast Janine Langer got the clippers out and gave each of the boys a crew cut, which included their number shaved into the back of their heads.

As Steve was getting his prized locks shorn, the Australian selectors were finalising the 22–man squad for the World Cup in England. Later that morning Steve and seven other Broncos heard of their selection – over the public address system at the club. This was yet another excuse for a beer or two, which they duly had. The eight were captured in serious celebration mode (Willie Carne had carelessly misplaced his shorts) in a photo in the *Courier-Mail* the following morning.

They were still in high spirits for the ticker-tape parade and public reception in King George Square later that week. Jim Soorley presented the team with the keys to the city. The crowd cheered. The players grinned.

The papers were full of stories and photos of the players. One photo captured Steve and Lis embracing just minutes after the final whistle in the Grand Final. They both knew exactly what it had taken to get there. There was also a shot of Steve with his seven-year-old nephew Donald Malone with the Grand Final trophy. There was even a horse race named in his honour. The first at Eagle Farm the following Saturday was the Steve Renouf/Chris Johns Handicap, appropriately a sprint.

Steve Ricketts produced a reflective piece for the *Courier-Mail*. 'Renouf said that his father's death from a heart attack in February made him all the more determined than ever to reach the top,' Ricketts reported, and then quoted Steve: 'Everything I did this year was for him.'

Too right.

When the Australians arrived in England for the World Cup, the Broncos contingent probably wished they had more hair. They had a couple of lead-up games, one against Huddersfield in Yorkshire. Wayne Bennett had played for the club and there was a photo of the lanky Queenslander on the clubhouse wall.

The Australians looked the goods. In those days the World Cup was a one-off match played between the two national teams regarded as the best in the world: at that time Australia and Great Britain. Competition for spots in the Kangaroos side was full-on. Steve got the nod. He would make his debut for Australia in the centres with Mal Meninga. 'To actually play alongside [Mal] in a game as important as the Wembley Cup Final can't even be described as a dream come true. It's better than that,' he later told *Rugby League Week*.

The final lacked the sparkle of a top-class rugby league contest. Both defences were on top, and trailing 4–6 with not more than ten minutes to go the Australians were beyond the worried stage. It was looking desperate.

'Not much was happening all game,' Steve recalls. 'Kevvy's come off the bench and he's gone "We'll do the *outball*" and I go "No, no. Bullshit. No." So I'm standing over there and the next thing I see him coming.'

The rest is history. Walters threw a classic long flat pass to Pearl, who was having a bludge down the left side. Pearl got on the outside of John Devereux, hit the pass with perfect timing, and strolled over for the try that won the World Cup.

Back in Australia Steve's try was replayed over and over and over, just as his Grand Final try had been. 'I credit that try to Kevvy,' Steve says, laughing, "cos I had no option. He made me do it. And we ended up scoring.'

Again the media seemed to focus on Steve Renouf. 'It's been a terrific year,' he told reporters, 'winning the premiership and making the Australian squad. Then I got to play my first international at Wembley where the atmosphere was unbelievable, but the biggest event of the year will definitely be [the birth of] the baby.' Lis had only weeks to go in her pregnancy.

In the meantime the rest of the Broncos arrived for the World Club Challenge – the match between the premier sides of Australia and Britain. The Broncos beat Wigan 22–8. Yet another trophy.

In just a few weeks Steve had become an absolute star of the game, indeed of Brisbane and Queensland life. He had no idea of the public profile that had developed in the month he was away in England. 'I was totally naive about that sort of thing,' he admits.

He was adored. The fans loved what he could do on a footy field. They warmed to his humility, to the fact that he was surprised to be receiving the accolades. They could relate to him: an ordinary young bloke whose family were so important to him.

Some fans were even moved to poetry. Glenda Barkle wrote 'For Bucko', which celebrated Steve's season and the memory of his father. It finished:

Well Bucko, I firmly believe Ol' Charlie would be proud,
Watching over all you'd done, maybe peeping over a cloud,
To see his youngest son amongst the best of them all,
Become a world class player, in his beloved football.

Soon after returning to Australia to be with Lis as she prepared for the birth, Steve received a phone call from Mick Retchless, the publican at the Royal Hotel in Murgon. 'We're having a bit of a do up here for you,' he said. 'Can you make it up?'

Steve and Lis travelled home to Murgon to find a huge celebration at the pub. 'I had no idea it was going to be like that,' he says. 'It showed to me how proud the town was.' The big banner read: WELL DONE BUCKO. WELCOME HOME. He was Bucko again.

People came from everywhere. His sisters from Brisbane. Family and friends from Murgon. There were drinks galore; a barbie; speeches. 'Steve was absolutely chuffed,' Sonia remembers. 'He'd had a few before he spoke and he just said a few thankyous.'

The party kicked on into the night. His old coach, Steve Button, reckons it was one of the best nights ever. 'Steve made a lot of people very proud,' Steve Button says. 'And there were a lot of non-Indigenous people saying that.' Steve had not snuck back into Murgon as a failed footballer, as some people had predicted. Five seasons had passed and he was returning a hero. Those who had dismissed him were now calling him one of their own.

It takes quite a lot to affect how people think. In his own unassuming way Bucko had done just that.

CHAPTER 8

Highs and Lows

A s STEVE HAD said, football had given him – and Lis – some wonderful moments, but none compared with the birth of their first child. Samuel Bruce Renouf was born at the Mater Mothers on 3 December 1992. The proud parents felt they were on their way towards building the family they so hoped for. This was what it was really about for Lis and Steve.

The birth of baby Sam meant something to lots of Queenslanders too. Steve's remarkable couple of months on the football field at the end of the 1992 season had catapulted him into the status of local celebrity, and people were keen to know more about him, and Lis. Sam's birth was news, and Steve and Lis were photographed with the little fella. 'Proud dad Steve doesn't show the same prowess handling his son that he does with a football,' the *Courier-Mail* story read. But he was 'definitely a doting dad'. The couple couldn't have looked happier. That's how they felt. Lis hoped to have another baby fairly quickly. Steve was adopting a wait-and-see attitude.

Things seemed to have changed very quickly after Steve's time in England. It was as if a few fleeting moments – the Grand Final try and the World Cup try – had been seen by so many people that he was suddenly famous; certainly a lot more famous than he had been. In the public imagination Steve Renouf had won the World Cup for Australia.

For Steve it would take some getting used to. Everything about him seemed to be of interest to the public. Over the months that followed, as well as being a regular in the newspapers, he appeared in calendars (looking casual with Mick Hancock, and oiled-up with Glen Lazarus), and did ads for radio and television.

The Broncos certainly understood the value of their classy centre, both on and off the football field. Steve had been playing under the terms of a contract he'd negotiated himself. But he was in demand, and the talk was that other clubs were after him – and were willing to pay. A story in the southern press claimed that Easts were very keen.

Not long after Steve's return from England the Broncos decided to circumvent any outside offers. John Ribot approached him, suggesting they upgrade his contract. While travelling together up to Mt Coot-tha to do an interview at Channel 7, Steve agreed to Ribot's offer.

In the days that followed Steve and Lis began to feel less than happy with the terms of the new contract. They had a sense that it undervalued him. Steve was a footballer, not a negotiator. He wasn't someone who thought much about the financial side of things. Lis was more astute in that area.

Steve called Ribot to request a further meeting. Ribot and Steve had always got on well. Ribot knew footy clubs struggled if the players were unhappy. But Ribot was also a company man. 'John Ribot had to side with the employer,' Steve explains. 'They're a business. So they'll try to get any player for as small an amount as they can. They're not going to come in and start by offering top dollar. They're going to start way down so they've got something to work with.'

Footballers are assets for clubs – on and off the field. They help them generate significant profits. They have an obvious value as players. But players like Steve, who are seen as decent, clean-living, family men, have a value in building the culture and the perceived culture of the club. The Broncos club was styling itself as the family club, and Steve fitted in perfectly with that image.

But how do you put a dollar value on footballers? For many years players in most professional sports, particularly the football codes, were underpaid in relation to club and league turnovers. They received tiny percentages while other parties benefited substantially, yet they were the ones creating the 'industry'. They were the key elements in the business's success. They made it happen.

Steve didn't think too much about that sort of thing, but he was learning. He was savvy enough to realise that a few well-chosen words to a couple of Sydney journalists might add a few dollars to his bank account. He and Lis also asked Geoff Bishop (Lis's uncle, who was involved in business, finance and investment) to sit in on any further meetings.

At the first meeting nothing had changed. Ribot repeated the offer made in the car. Steve was not willing to sign on the spot. He and Geoff asked for more time.

Shortly after, something stirred the Broncos into action. It may have been the paper-talk doing the rounds. 'When we went back,' Steve recalls, 'it was totally different. Ribes just pulled out a new contract and said, "What do you think about that?" We looked at it and went, "That's more like it."'

It was a great deal: substantial six-figure numbers over three years. Steve couldn't find a pen quickly enough. And all for playing football. The details of the arrangement included a position as a sales and marketing cadet at Australia Post, one of the Broncos sponsors. Steve liked the security of a long-term career path out-side of football, but the deal had its down-side. The new contract meant leaving the Mater. Steve felt very awkward about that. As a rule, no apprentices were kept on at the Mater after finishing their time. But the boys in the workshop had signed a petition to have Steve continue, and the administration had agreed to make an exception. He now had to tell them he was going to be a marketing whiz at the post office. People at the Mater were disappointed, but they wished him well.

They knew there were big things in store for Steve.

Public notoriety didn't make Kelvin Giles' pre-season orders any easier to carry out. However, Steve was spared some of the slog of another summer preparation, by injury. Increasingly, professional footballers were booked in for minor patch-up surgery during the break. It was like being sent off to the mechanic to get an end-of-year service and tune. During the second half of the 1992 season Steve had put up with a niggly groin injury; it was not serious enough to cause him to miss games, nor enough to need injections to play, but it was painful enough to be disconcerting. Most professional footballers carry some ongoing problem but have to deal with the pain. They just have to find a way to shut it out.

With the extended international campaign the injury had deteriorated. If he laughed, it hurt. If he coughed, he actually had to hold his groin – which wasn't a good look.

The January operation to stretch a tendon in his groin seemed to be successful. But the injury wouldn't heal and then infection set in. Steve started to feel quite unwell. One night back home at Bruce and Jenny's place he nearly fainted. He started to lose weight noticeably. He lost nearly 10 kilograms in a fortnight or so. He had no energy. He knew there was a problem but he wouldn't visit the doctor. He thought it was something sinister and he didn't want to know about it.

Still working at the Mater at this stage, he was becoming irritable, which, according to John Hunter, wasn't like Steve at all. Concerned for Steve's health, Hunter invited him over to his home in Buranda, where he kept and trained a couple of grey-hounds. He persuaded Steve to pee on a piece of litmus paper to test his sugar level. The paper went an awful brown.

Hunter had a friend with blood-sugar problems who had completed the same litmus test, so he had a pretty good idea of what was wrong. They went straight to the Wesley Hospital where Steve was admitted. His wayward biochemistry had put him close to collapse.

Steve Renouf, on top of the world, a new dad, and building to the height of his footballing powers, was diagnosed as having diabetes. What did it all mean? Was this it?

Steve and Lis and Wayne Bennett had worked so hard to build his career, and Steve finally felt he belonged at the top level. Respected commentators were describing him as one of the game's premier players. He had confronted the doubt that had troubled him. He believed he could mix it with the best. And now this?

He lay alone in hospital wondering whether it was all going to be taken away? And wondering what he would do? And what about Sam and Lis?

He knew what diabetes was, but he had little idea of what the disorder meant for his health and lifestyle, let alone what it meant for football. He knew it was a serious disease, and he thought it was bad. Really bad. But, like anything, it was a matter of coming to understand it, casting off the prejudices about the condition, and working within the constraints it would place on him.

He explained his reaction to *Rugby League News* in their first State of Origin edition later that year: 'That was a pretty touch and go time for me. At one stage I thought I was a bit iffy about ever playing football again. But there are a lot of misconceptions about what diabetes really is and what limitations it imposes. The truth is, when it all boils down, if you follow a correct diet and your doctor's advice, there is nothing you can't do.' Steve adjusted to his insulin-dependent lifestyle quickly. He has since relied on four self-administered injections every day.

It is not in Steve's nature to resent what life dishes out. It is, for Steve, *life*. And his team-mates noticed that. Steve's determination not to let diabetes interfere with his career won him even more respect. At the launch of the 1993 season Glen Lazarus sang Steve's praises, referring to the diagnosis. 'You talk about courage and toughness, don't go past Steve Renouf,' he said. Lazarus also referred to the way Steve had dealt with the loss of his father over the previous twelve months.

Steve could always find the good in things, and even diabetes had a benefit. He now had a perfect alibi at training, although it meant he was always on the receiving end from the Ipswich boys. If Steve was off with the fairies, being more vague than usual, Alfie would say, 'Will someone get Pearl a few jelly babies?' or 'Pearl, git over there an' have a can'o'Coke.'

The media became preoccupied with Steve's condition. He gave repeated assurances he would be fine. His performances certainly didn't suffer. He started the season where he'd finished in 1992. He had become an established player, a centre who knew the ropes. He had been named as one of the five NRL Players of the 1992 season, along with Glen Lazarus and Allan Langer. And he was ready to fire up again.

Just as the season was kicking off, there was a serious incident back home in Murgon. The local publican, Dermot Tiernan, was killed in a brawl outside his Australian Hotel, the very pub where Nan South had worked for all those years.

Steve was saddened by the tragedy. He loved Murgon, often defending it, speaking out against claims that it was a town haunted by racial problems. Yet he also believed that violence was all too prevalent there. And now someone was dead.

Football didn't seem very important by comparison.

During the off-season there were changes to football in Brisbane. After an acrimonious dispute with the Queensland Rugby League, the Broncos settled on a deal with the Brisbane City Council to make the QE II Stadium their home ground. Some fans weren't too impressed: Lang Park was considered the home of rugby league in Queensland.

But, as was Steve's way, he just accepted the decision and got on with life. 'I was a bit disappointed,' he recalls, 'but I accepted any decision the club made. I kept away from that sort of stuff. I was never outspoken. I was a bit of a sheep like that.' Steve grew to love the fast track, which became known as ANZ Stadium.

The new venue could hold around 55,000 people, and, with Brisbane the team to beat again in 1993, the Broncos board knew that often it would be filled to near-capacity. Despite initial organisational problems, the board was right. People flocked to ANZ to support the Broncos in the pleasant winter sunshine.

Notorious slow-starters, Brisbane were again up and down in the opening rounds of the season. Any suggestion they were invincible was soon dispelled by a loss to Canterbury in Round 2. The following week the Eels spoiled the party in the first game at ANZ.

The Broncos needed to beat St George in the Round 7 match at Kogarah. The Grand Final replay was tight throughout, but it was a bit of Renouf magic that made the difference. With the score locked at 14–14 he scored the match-winning try.

Good judges were starting to make comparisons with the great

Good times: Steve with
Wayne Bennett (joyful
smirk) after the 1992
Grand Final.
(*Rugby League Week*,
John Elliott)

Not so good times: Steve
with Wayne Bennett
(troubled smirk) during
the 1997 Tri-Series final,
Queensland v New
South Wales, at ANZ
Stadium.
(*Courier-Mail*)

Rather versatile: the Broncos centres in 1994. Keeping the sponsors happy, singing the new team song 'Broncos for Queensland' as exactly half a barber's shop quartet. (*Courier-Mail*, Geoff McLachlan)

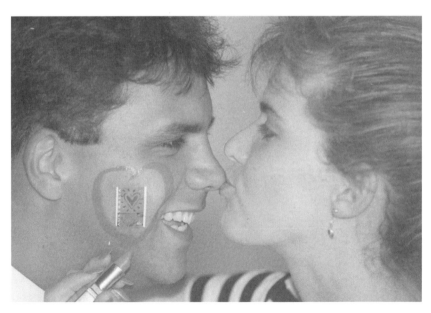

The loyal employee: promoting the new Valentine's Day stamp with Lis for Australia Post in February 1995. (*Courier-Mail*)

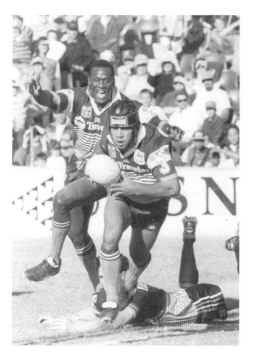

Missed him again. Steve left many tacklers clutching at the air. This time he beats his Penrith opponent much to the delight of Wendell Sailor (with hair), 1995.
(*Courier-Mail*)

In full flight. And the fend about to arrive, strong and perfectly timed to accelerate off the defender, Ken Nagus, in a match against Canberra, 1996.
(*Courier-Mail*, Geoff McLachlan)

No nerves today: Steve with the fans during the Super League Grand Final parade in Brisbane, September 1997. (*Courier-Mail*, Anthony Weate)

Like an Olympic 200m runner: powering away on a typical Steve Renouf arc during the 1997 Tri-Series final, Queensland v New South Wales, at ANZ Stadium. How quick was he? 'As quick as I needed to be,' Steve always said. (*Courier-Mail*, Anthony Weate)

Attack came naturally. Four tries was more than enough for the Man of the Match award against Canterbury at ANZ Stadium in 1993. After his final try, Steve shrugged his shoulders at Mick Hancock: 'How did I do that?' (*Courier-Mail*, Geoff McLachlan)

But defence, Steve had to work at. Eventually it came, as this tackle below suggests. Steve hammers Sid Domic in the Broncos Round 3 clash against Penrith in 1998. (*Courier-Mail*, Simon Renilson)

Pearl celebrating? One of the few times Steve showed unrestrained
jubilation after scoring against Cronulla in the Super League Grand Final
in 1997. Kevvy looks pretty happy, if not a little surprised, as do Wendell
Sailor (no hair) and Anthony Mundine. (*Courier-Mail*, Bruce Long)

The boys. They spent a lot of time together over 10 years, and here was
another celebration, just after the 1998 Grand Final victory against
Canterbury. (*Courier-Mail*, David Kapernick)

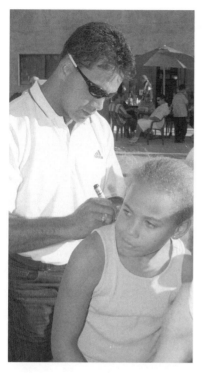

Steve, working for the community. Here, with 11-year-old Hannah Geesu, helping to promote an Indigenous employment initiative, in Maryborough. (*Fraser Coast Chronicle*, Sonia Sutcliffe)

Comeback: still drawing big crowds while playing for Easts in 2004. (*Courier-Mail*, Annette Dew)

The Renoufs in England with Andrew Gee, and Rob (Broncos physio) and Amanda Godbolt and kids.

Family Renouf at home and settled: Freddie, Lis, Sunita, Sam, Charlie (gripping seat), Billy, Steve and Ellie the dog.
(*Courier-Mail*, Anthony Weate)

centres. Journalists often referred to Steve as 'the classy centre' or 'the prince of centres'. They also noted the improvement in his defensive skills.

Steve was an automatic selection for Queensland. As the squad gathered for another camp, the papers were full of Origin. Renouf was the star. He would be, the writers thought, one of the keys to Maroon success.

Again, Steve could feel the weight of expectation on him. On the day of the match he felt tense and apprehensive. He liked the playing part of Origin, especially as he was partnering Meninga in the centres again, but he didn't enjoy the pressure in the build-up.

As he sat in the Lang Park dressing room on the night of the match, he rang Paul Bishop, who was in his customary position behind the bar in his lounge-room on the pig farm outside Murgon. Bish could feel Bucko's tension. He sounded timid, almost lost. 'I'd rather be up there with you fellas,' Steve half-joked. 'Hang on,' Bish replied, 'we'll send a chopper down to get you.'

That night another tight match unfolded. It was last-man-standing stuff. And all Steve seemed to do was defend, until late in the first half the full weight of opponent Paul McGregor landed across his foot. It looked totally innocuous, but at the instant of contact Steve's foot was on its side. A lot of damage had been done and the injury (known as a lisfranc sprain) was very painful. The Blues won 14–10 and Steve was out of the next Origin side.

The Broncos had their same old mid-season problems. The club competition was fairly even and they had eleven players with State of Origin commitments. Some of the usual Reserve Graders, like John Plath, were influencing games, but the team was just treading water. Even when the full side ran on, their form was inconsistent.

It improved, and a lot of that was thanks to Steve. He was given plenty of room to move by the strong performance of the work-horse pack led by Lazarus, Gee, Hohn and Gillmeister. That was all he needed. In Round 14 he cut Souths up, helping the Broncos to a 54–8 victory. Channel 9 commentator Ray Warren was at his sing-song best. When Steve flashed onto a pass, Ray exploded, 'Renouf!' Then he chanted with the rhythm of Steve's movement: 'In and away. Out and away. Down she goes. Renouf.' You could tell how brilliant Rabs thought it was from his call. And people were left smiling and shaking their heads in lounge-rooms everywhere.

A fortnight later Steve scored three tries in a close, high-scoring game against Cronulla, which the Broncos won 38–34. Then the following week he put in one of his best-ever per-formances, scoring four tries in the 38–18 win over premiership rival, Canterbury. It was one of those days. His body was good. His mind was clear. He felt fantastic. And things just happened out there. After crossing for his fourth try, Steve was walking back to hand the football to Terry Matterson when he caught the eye of Mick Hancock. Steve just shrugged his shoulders and put his hands out, palms up, a gesture which said, 'How did I do that? Where does it come from?' Hancock laughed. Steve smiled. It was typical Renouf. He expressed himself through movement but even he wasn't sure how it happened.

The fans just kept applauding. How good was this bloke? Reporters had the thesaurus out looking for the right words to describe him. Bennett could no longer keep a lid on it. He said at the media conference after the game, 'Steve is up there with the really great centres to have played the game, when he is on.' Bennett still remembers Steve's performance that day.

Paul Malone was pretty impressed as well. 'Steve Renouf is on the verge of being one of the all-time greats of rugby league,' he wrote in the *Courier-Mail*. 'Comparisons to a name like Reg Gasnier are carried out at your own peril, but over the past twelve months Renouf has developed before our eyes into a tackle-breaker and runner of rare quality.' He supported his case by listing Steve's attributes: acceleration, deception, a monster fend, brute strength, and opportunism.

The following week the Broncos beat Parramatta 15–4, and looked to be rampaging into the finals when they travelled to Canberra. It was a bitterly cold Friday night. The Broncos shivered as the frost descended on Bruce Stadium. Playing to secure a spot in the top three, they were thrashed. Mal Meninga scored an intercept try which sealed the game: Canberra 20, Brisbane 4. Steve had one of the worst games of his entire career. He missed a number of crucial tackles, and just couldn't get into the game in attack.

Being a Friday-night game in the dead of winter, half of Queensland was sitting in front of the TV in fleecie-lined tracky dacks and ugg boots, heater cranked to the max, watching the footy. And, as brilliant as Steve had been in the previous month, they began asking those same questions about his defence again. It doesn't take much for some fans to drop off.

Steve knew he'd had a shocker and he was embarrassed. He felt he'd let his team-mates down. And he'd performed poorly in front of the opponent he most respected: Mal. The players noticed. And of course the coach noticed. 'He knew the team were pissed off with him,' Bennett recalls. 'I knew the team were pissed off with him. A couple came up to me and said "What about Steve's performance? He let us down." And he was woeful.' But Bennett didn't say anything, as he explains: 'I learnt pretty early on that criticism never helped Steve Renouf. I knew I had to address it but I let it go. We got to the team meeting on Monday and Steve grabbed me and said "I want to say something". Steve had never put his hand up at a team meeting before that.'

You could imagine Alf and Kevvy looking at each other in the Monday meeting: 'What's goin' on here? Pearl's got his hand up.' Steve spoke briefly. It was one of the toughest things he had ever done. He wasn't a big talker. And he hated facing difficult situations. 'I was shattered,' he explains, 'but it was something I felt I had to do. I needed to say something, to tell them that I didn't mean to play like that.' His apology came from the heart. It won him even more respect. 'As we were leaving the room,' Bennett recalls, 'all those guys who were wanting to hang him were coming up and asking, "Can you help Steve? Can we do anything?" I just said, "He don't need no help. He just had a bad night."'

It was a long wait for the next match, and Steve tried to redeem himself at training. He was flying. 'I could tell from our last training session that we were going to have a good game,' he recalls. He felt good.

The Round 20 clash was against the battling Balmain at ANZ Stadium. Another Friday night; another big television audience. In the preview, Steve's poor defensive game against Canberra was singled out. Fatty Vautin described it as 'a bit dusty'. Gene Miles told viewers the Broncos had had a problem with defending the left side of the field but it had been addressed during the week.

The problem didn't appear to have been addressed in the first quarter of an hour, when the Broncos missed a dozen tackles. Three of those misses came in the opening set of six. Cans were flung at Rank Arenas all around Queensland. But Balmain didn't make the most of their early opportunities and the Broncos worked their way back into the game. Pearl was at his mercurial best. When Kevin Walters sent him a textbook outball he had Tiger centre Jacin Sinclair absolutely bamboozled. He was pointing and sliding and calling, but Steve had him beaten. You could see it all unfolding and Steve burst through the tiniest of gaps, bolted 30 metres, got to Tim Brasher, stood in the tackle, and did a full 360 while waiting for a runner. Kevvy arrived to take Pearl's pass. Then he rifled one to his brother Kerrod, who flipped a short ball off his hip to Terry Matterson on the burst. Over. Superb try.

Soon after, the Broncos had an overlap. Quick hands. Steve: the final pass to Willie Carne. In, in the corner. Minutes later and Steve runs off Matterson. Sprints 20 metres. Takes the cover towards the touchline. Looks outside. No Mick Hancock. Hears the voice inside. At full pace he floats one back over his right shoulder to nothing more than the voice of Hancock, who doesn't have to break stride. Over.

The Broncos lead 20–0 at half-time and Steve's confidence is sky-high. Straightaway, he breaks the line. His movements are just too sharp. His footwork seems to tie his opponents feet in knots and they fall around him like it's a choreographed slapstick per-formance, as if the script says, 'The Keystone Cops go arse-up'. He comes to the full-back and grubbers ahead. It's well-weighted. He'll score. But he doesn't, because Morvyn Edwards takes him out. Penalty. The commentators play his line-break over and over.

Has Steve learnt to do that? You can't teach that sort of bal-ance. The instinct that leads the body to make those decisions can't be described. You have to see it. Where does it come from? Is it an Aboriginal understanding of space? Or was it a skill learned in those games of touch back in Murgon? Steve was able to make the spectacular and risky appear ordinary and natural.

Minutes later and yet again Renouf gets through. He looks to be taking a ball on the outside of his opponent but at the last instant switches inside and in a step-and-a-half seems to be a mile from the angle he began running. No one touches him as he glides through. Breaks the line. Gets away. Beats two. Palms another defender off. Steps out of a tackle. Swerves infield. Lets the full-back tackle him. Gets his arms free (all at absolute full throttle) and turns a regulation pass inside to Hancock who strolls over. Fatty can't contain himself. When he finally gets the mike off Sterlo, he says, 'Renouf is a freak; an absolute freak.'

But there's more to come. Kerrod Walters swoops on a loose ball near his own 22, sprints straight across field to link up with Pearl, who hits the ball at right angles and at top pace – and they don't get near him. It's late in the game but his acceleration 10 metres after he gets the ball is eye-catching. It is his fifteenth try of the season, equalling his own record for most tries in a season at the Broncos. And there's still more, as Pearl stands the defence up, explodes away and puts Hancock over again. The Broncos win 50–0. Steve has had an absolute blinder.

It was a very satisfying performance for Steve. Footballers rot in the purgatory of the week that follows a poor performance. But they do have the chance to redeem themselves. Canberra seemed a long time ago.

He had the whole weekend free. He was going back to Murgon for Steve Button junior's 21st birthday party. For the first time ever, Lis decided not to go up with him. She and Sam would take it easy at home.

Steve was in good spirits – the sort of high a top-class sporting performance like his game against the Tigers can bring. As always, it was good to see friends and family. Everyone seemed to be enjoying the party, which, like all parties, had its share of laughs and beers, when things got a bit heated.

Steve recalls the incident:

I was standing at the bar having a chat with a few of the boys. Debbie, my sister, came running towards me. She'd been having an argument with Frank [Malone]. And he came after her. I don't know what had happened before, but blood's thicker than water, and in protecting Debbie, Frank and I had a bit of a scuffle. Which was unusual. I mean Frank and I go way back. We love each other. It was weird. We cleared it that night. We apologised, made up, had a beer together. And Frank was sweet with it . . . As far as I knew, it was over.

Steve went home to Palmer Street, where he was staying, and next morning a few car loads of Frank's sisters and nephews arrived. Steve explains what happened next:

I went out to see what was going on. There would have been more than a dozen people standing on the footpath. I walked out and said, 'What do you want?' There were four guys standing in front of me in a sort of arc. I knew all four of them. They said, 'We heard you got into Frank last night; that you kicked the shit out of Frank.' I said, 'No. Nothing like that happened at all. You've got it wrong.'

They were all drunk. They got the story from Frank's sisters. They're the ones who told these young fellas what had happened. They were all around and someone said something and I turned to see what he had to say and next thing I got king-hit from the other side. I was nervous going out there, but I wasn't expecting that.

There was an angry altercation and the fence at 31 Palmer Street was pushed over. Mrs Renouf had seen her son being hit and she reacted wildly. 'She just went off,' Steve says. 'They had to hold her back. I've never seen her like that before. She was so upset.' Steve knew straightaway that his jaw was broken.

Steve didn't ring Lis. He didn't know how to tell her. He knew he had to face her, and explain what had happened, and he knew it would upset her, even trouble her. He hated that. He didn't want it to be like that.

He couldn't face telling Wayne Bennett either. He was going to be out for the season for sure. How do you tell a coach who has nurtured you, who has shown great faith in you, and who needs you on the paddock, that you've been injured in a Sunday morning blue? And then convince him it wasn't your fault? What would his team-mates say? And the media? What would they do with a story like this? For a Queensland audience, bottle-fed rugby league and the Broncos on a daily basis, it would be one of the biggest stories of the year. The more he thought about it, the worse he felt. It was an absolute disaster.

Steve rang Kelvin Giles. He had sought no medical attention in Murgon and he asked Giles to organise a doctor in Brisbane. He also asked him to tell Bennett. Steve just couldn't bring himself to do that.

He reported the incident to the police (who eventually pressed charges), before heading back to Brisbane. His nephews drove him in his car. Steve sat in the passenger's seat holding his jaw, every bump reverberating through the fractures. He was at once angry and sad, wounded and upset, dispirited.

So much was going through his mind. Here he was trying to do his small part to break down a widely held view of Aboriginal people, and he had been assaulted by one of them. Steve had always believed that confrontation and conflict did not resolve anything. Old Charlie had been very strong on that. But there were plenty of Aboriginal people who didn't share his views. 'There has always been a culture of violence up there,' Steve reflects. 'The Cherbourg footy team just now [2004] after three years has been let back into the comp. They were kicked out because of violence.'

Steve had seen the sort of incident he was unwittingly

involved in many times over the years. 'I grew up with that sort of thing,' he says sadly. 'A family member might get in a blue, but then you have to fight the whole lot of them. That's just the way it was. And no one ever does anything about it. No one goes to the police. And then people would turn around and complain when it just kept happening. I thought: do something about it. It's wrong. What gives people the right to blue whoever they want? Too much is let go, and then it happens again, and again. So I went to the police.'

The young culprit was eventually convicted. 'In the end I felt sorry for the bloke because he would have been gee-ed up to do it. I don't think he had any idea of what had gone on the night before. It was second-hand news and it was pepped up and he was full of bravado and grog.'

Steve had surgery immediately. Although titanium plates were inserted, the jaw didn't have to be wired. There was a possibility he could be back playing in six weeks, which would be about the time of the Grand Final.

News spread quickly. Chris Johns heard of the incident on a radio news bulletin on the Sunday morning. 'I couldn't believe it,' he recalls. 'The minute I heard it I knew it wouldn't have been Steve's fault. Because he wasn't a big drinker and he didn't have an aggressive bone in his body. There were others who may have got themselves in strife, but not Steve.' He went straight to the hospital to see how Steve was and found a broken young man. Johns wanted to head up to Murgon and sort things out. Steve told him to 'just let it go'.

Bennett visited Steve a couple of days later at home. He could feel the young man's disappointment. He shared it. Steve had been worried about what his coach's reaction would be, but Bennett is a wise man. 'I never made him feel guilty,' he says.

Steve was relieved. 'Wayne understood. He made me feel OK.'

Steve recalls what Bennett said: 'No one's blaming you for what happened. We're behind you. You get that jaw fixed and I'll put you straight back in the team. Don't worry about it.'

The *Courier-Mail* didn't sensationalise the incident. 'They looked after me,' Steve says. The incident hardly rated a mention, but there were rumours. Bennett briefed the players on the Monday morning. Heads dropped. The boys were sorry for one of their own, and for the effect his absence might have. As good an all-round team as the Broncos had, Pearl's spark would be missed.

Stories did the rounds. There was talk about what had happened, and what sort of bloke Steve Renouf was. Wayne Bennett wasn't impressed, and he set things straight in his *Courier-Mail* column:

> By now it is certain that rumours and theories will have spread like wildfire about how Steve Renouf broke his jaw. Depending on who you listen to, he might have been painted as an aggressive person, a big-head or someone who can get himself into trouble when the drinks start to multiply and the night gets longer. So often the public gets a distorted opinion of a champion player . . . As his coach of six years I want to tell you that Steve Renouf is none of those things and I can tell you what type of person he is. Apart from being one of the most exciting players I have seen, this Broncos centre is one of the finest young men I have been involved with.

It is easy for a footballer to feel on the outer while sidelined with a long-term injury, particularly if the injury is sustained in controversial circumstances. Steve just wanted to get back as quickly as possible, and was soon on the paddock. Kelvin Giles was delighted with his progress. He told *Rugby League Week*: 'It was great to see Steve at training last week. There he was with his fat little frog face handling the football again, doing some light running and a few drills. He was back with his pals in the environment that has become a special part of his life. The sparkle was back – you could see it in his eyes. When you have to sit at home and dwell on the negatives it eats away at you.'

The jaw was healing well and it wasn't long before he could do the ball-work as well, as long as the klutzes at the Broncos didn't bump into him.

The Broncos drew on their depth. Willie Carne moved into the centres and a young Wendell Sailor was given his chance. Both performed solidly. The Broncos could have finished on top of the ladder had they beaten premiership favourites St George at ANZ in the final round. They lost 10–16 and such was the evenness of the competition that they finished fifth, two points off top spot. It would be a task to win the flag from there, but they found some ominous form in the first two weeks of the finals, beating Manly and Canberra.

It was a bitter-sweet situation for Steve. He was pleased for the team, but was desperate to be part of it. 'Some of the games that the boys played,' he recalls, 'they just whopped their opponents – good sides. They whopped Manly . . . They scored some great tries. That made me even hungrier. I wanted to be back in the team.'

Part of Steve's time in waiting was spent in a new role as a *Courier-Mail* columnist where, in typical Steve style, he wrote it as he saw it. Over the years Steve had benefited from Kevin Walters' ability to read a situation and then execute the right play, and although Walters had never been rated a superstar in the south, Steve was adamant that this was exactly what he was. Following Kevvy's superb performance in which he set up the victory against Manly, Steve wrote: 'I don't think it is widely appreciated how good a player Kevin is. So it will surprise some when I rate him as one of the top five players in the world when he is firing like that . . . I would have given anything to have played outside him in that sort of form. Certainly Willie Carne picked the right time to come in closer to Kevin's supply line.'

In preliminary final week the medical reports were favourable and Steve looked a real chance to play. But he had to prove to Bennett he was ready. There was no way the coach would risk a fragile player against the hardened Canterbury unit. Steve showed no signs of the injury during the Tuesday run, but Bennett had one last test for him. After the rest had finished training, he had Gaven Allen run straight at Steve several times. Steve knocked him over each time. Then Bennett called Allen over for a chat. There was to be one last go. Allen ran hard and Steve got him low, dropped him, and fell with the prop's weight, in a copybook tackle. As Allen got up, he pushed his forearm firmly into Steve's face just to see how he was going. The coach made a mental note that Steve didn't flinch.

It was the big question in football: should the Broncos risk Steve Renouf? There were theories everywhere: pub theories, cabbies' theories, talkback theories. But Bennett was confident, and Steve was picked. Pearl was back.

Steve wore the No. 30 jumper for the preliminary final. The Broncos kicked off and in the first set Martin Bella attacked up Steve's side of the field. They were certain to test him out. The talk had been that there'd be a bit of rough stuff as well.

Steve was a little apprehensive. There was plenty on his mind, but he was as determined in the opening minutes of that match as he had ever been. The Broncos were close to the line when the ball went left. Kevvy sent a pass to Steve who double-jinked, palmed away a tackler, and dived over in the corner. It was his first touch for the match. The Broncos led and Steve had found some confidence. It turned into a memorable final. At 16–16 for much of the second half and with the crowd going wild, Steve got free and took off down the left. He came to the full-back. In and away, moving as beautifully as ever. It looked like he just had to dive for the corner to score – and normally he probably would have launched himself at the line. But he was for once rather cautious and chose to turn the ball back inside to Hancock. It floated forward. No try. The Broncos rallied and, as rare as it was, Langer kicked a field goal to break the deadlock, before Alan Cann went over to make the final score 23–16. The Broncos would have a chance to defend their premiership.

It was a deeply satisfying day for Steve Renouf. His team-mates acknowledged his courage and his determination. His coach was absolutely delighted. These were the moments Bennett savoured most: young people facing a test and coming through. 'He played magnificently in that game,' Wayne Bennett says with fatherly pride. 'It was Steve's way of telling everyone he appreciated their support and them sticking with him. That was Steve.'

Again Bennett encouraged his players to enjoy the week of the Grand Final, to taste every minute of it. Again the Broncos would play St George and again the match took on a Queensland versus New South Wales focus. Neutral commentators could find an argument for both sides: Brisbane's cavalier style against the Dragons' structure and discipline.

It was the Tina Turner Grand Final. She belted out 'Simply the Best' as the boys readied themselves in the sheds. Once out on the paddock, Steve found himself under intense physical pressure, particularly from the robust St George centre Graeme Bradley. But the Broncos were steady, and just too good again, scoring three tries to nil in the 14–6 victory. They'd won four times in September to become premiers.

With the 1992 win the players had been excited and jubilant, but Steve remembers everyone being more relieved than anything else in 1993. Willie Carne sat on his haunches and shed a few tears. It had all been very draining.

The fans, however, were no less jubilant and wanted to be part of the same celebration rituals as the previous year. The airport was rocking again, as was King George Square, then back to the club.

The players even lined up for the premiership crew cuts again.

With the successful season over, Lis and Steve decided to take a break from Brisbane. They had always wanted to see Uluru so they joined a tour group for a trip to central Australia. 'It was magnificent. Beautiful. Awe-inspiring,' Steve says. 'I felt a real sense of connection; the same sense I feel now when I visit the [Aboriginal] communities.'

The trip also gave them an opportunity to meet some of the local Aboriginal people. 'They didn't recognise me as an Aboriginal person,' Steve explains. 'And I didn't say anything. They were speaking in their own language. And giggling. They were probably giving it to us!'

The locals shared some bush tucker with them and then showed the tourists how to throw a spear with a woomera. Steve was invited to have a go and he sent it flying away into the distance. The locals were impressed. It was only then that Steve said, 'I should know how to do that. I *am* Aboriginal!'

Steve and Lis got to know a local teacher and he helped them get permission to visit one of the nearby Aboriginal communities. 'It was a real eye-opener,' Steve confides.

It was at moments like these, standing in the heart of the

Continent, away from the day-to-day demands of professional football, that Steve started to really think about what it meant to be an Aboriginal Australian.

For Steve, being able to handle a woomera was a very small part of it.

CHAPTER 9

Established

By THE EARLY 1990s rugby league had become a significant commercial enterprise. Some businessmen had always been involved with rugby league as players and supporters, and for them building a commercial relationship with the sport they loved was a happy marriage of work and play. Other operators looked at football as nothing more than a commercial opportunity. For them the game was arbitrary, and they sought to manipulate it for their own financial gain.

Steve loved to play football. He would have played in whichever competition was available to him. To be paid for it was a bonus, and he was happy to make the most of it. Lis understood that Steve loved performing on the field, but she was also aware that top-level football provided a way of securing the economic future of the young Renouf family.

For the vast audience of loyal supporters, football was much more than a business. It was part of their lives. Football meant a lot to them. Every year, they hoped it would be their team's season. Throughout much of rugby league's history people had barracked for the team of their local suburb or town in a local competition. If you were born and raised in Balmain, there was a pretty good chance you'd be a Tiger. For years it was the game that mattered. Footy had a long and rich history and had a meaningful place in the broader culture. People loved it – as it was.

But football was changing, and many people felt powerless in the face of that change. Entrepreneurs knew that football could work for them. They became involved in the decision-making processes at football clubs both directly and through commercial pressure, thereby helping to take football in the direction that best suited them. The clubs had significant budgets. And other businesses could see how they would be advantaged by building commercial relationships with rugby league. They became sponsors and advertisers.

Astute business people understood that football fans are consumers. We eat. We drink. We smoke. We drive. We watch TV. We listen to the radio. We read the papers. And so businesses started to associate their product with rugby league. Consider the 1993 Grand Final. It was played for the Winfield Cup, sponsored by a cigarette company, between a team sponsored by Power's, a beer company, and Penfold's, a wine company. Clearly someone thought rugby league fans were drinkers and smokers.

Increasingly, club administrators were thinking of football as a *product*, and those members of the public who had followed the game for years were *the market*. More and more we were hearing statements from football people which sounded like they were coming from hamburger chain executives: 'We have to grow the market to survive in the competitive world.'

The Broncos were always looking to build their sponsorship portfolio. At a cocktail party in Brisbane in late 1993, Paul 'Porky' Morgan met the media baron Rupert Murdoch, whose company, News Limited, had interests throughout the world. News Ltd owned (and still owns) the *Courier-Mail*. From that social function, a relationship between the two men developed and the biggest sponsorship deal in rugby league history was signed. It was worth $2 million annually. The only newspaper in town sponsored the only Australian Rugby League club in town. It was a sweet deal.

Because of their popularity, the Broncos already dominated the sports pages of the newspaper, and such is the nature of the cycle that this in turn helped to build their popularity. With a formal commercial relationship in place, the newspaper gave the Broncos even greater coverage. Steve's mates at the Mater Hospital called it the 'Bronco Mail'.

Steve and Chris Johns appeared in a photograph announcing and promoting the new sponsorship. John Ribot was quoted as saying, 'To have someone like Rupert Murdoch involved with our organisation is very exciting and just seeing the calibre of companies he has involvement in will take us to another dimension in our game.' One of those companies was a global pay-TV network. If Australian rugby league made it onto Sky TV in Britain, the Broncos would be able to sign even more lucrative sponsorship deals from major companies there. There were 10 million consumers in Queensland and New South Wales; there were 70 million in Britain. Who knew how many might tune in around the world? There was the chance that one day Steve would be playing for the Bovril Broncos, watched by new rugby league fans throughout Asia.

The deal with News Ltd also made the Broncos attractive to other sponsors, who knew stories regarding their product were likely to appear in the paper under the guise of news – which is exactly what happened. And so Steve and his team-mates, especially Alf, appeared in story after story. They became celebrity footballers.

Steve didn't crave public attention, although he always enjoyed the accolades football brought. He didn't want the spotlight. Chris Johns says, 'A lot of player go out there to *try* to get recognition. But Pearl didn't do that. He played footy because he just liked having a good game of footy.'

Yet he often featured in the paper. Steve was a loyal employee who felt an obligation to do the things that the club, Australia Post and the *Courier-Mail* asked of him. So he was photographed with Australia Post's series of matchbox cars in the team colours, with Lis on the release of a Valentine's Day stamp, with stamps stuck all over his face and a young fan holding a magnifying glass, with Chris Johns wearing a boater (emblazoned with the banner of the *Courier-Mail* and another sponsor, Traveland) and singing 'Broncos for Queensland'. There was a beefcake photo of him, bare-chested, as he looked into the distance, and a story about him picking up his Holden Commodore Club Sports car on loan from Zupps (Steve's personal sponsor, and also a club sponsor). There was a photo of him wearing Maddison headgear and advocating protection for kids, a photo of him wearing a huge bow-tie to promote Bow-Tie Friday, a photo with a young violinist (Suzi Thompson) from the Queensland Youth Symphony Orchestra.

These were often front-page stories which not only gave Steve a prominent position in the life of the state but helped to portray the Broncos as a community-minded club, a club which was part of the fabric of Brisbane and Queensland life.

Steve was also often photographed with Lis and Sam, who by then was very much the cute toddler. Steve was the family man. Lis reckons this was an accurate portrayal: that Steve has always put family first (and that he really was very good at changing nappies and being a real dad). And the Broncos were the family club. One fantastic photo of Steve with Sam in the bath by Geoff McLachlan generated quite a reaction. It flew in the face of the stereotype of wild, rugged, apish football players. But that was Steve. In many ways he was a little different in the football world.

The photo prompted comment from one academic, Peter West, who wrote: 'There is so much stuff about men in the media, most of it negative: blood-stained warriors, serial killers and so on. It's great to see someone promoting positive images of a man with his baby.'

As well, of course, there were the football photos. After the *Courier-Mail* became a sponsor, there was usually a front-page photo from the weekend's match. Being a prolific try-scorer, Steve often featured. Steve reckons someone at the *Courier-Mail* must have liked him. Liked him? He was worth squillions to them.

The sponsorship had had the desired effect. The symbiotic relationship between sporting club and media outlet was up and running productively. A new market was found, if not created. People who had never followed rugby league closely, indeed some never at all, now took an interest in it. They would never have gone looking for the coverage of rugby league in the past, but now it was being thrust in front of them. They were eating their Coco-Pops and scrambling through their homework, scoffing their bacon and eggs and taking their angina tablets, with Steve Renouf.

He was a character in their lives now. And so was his family. Steve and Lis had enjoyed the summer with Sam, quite the little character, and were expecting their second child in May. Until then, there were footy matches to play.

When the 1994 season got under way, the focus was on the Broncos, yet again, as they tried to win their third premiership in a row. Steve had an inauspicious start to the year when, in the opening round, he was cited for a spear tackle on Brett Plowman in the 16-all draw with Parramatta. He and Kerrod Walters had gone in to tackle the big Eels' winger and Steve managed to get his hand between Plowman's legs. Plowman's size and momentum flipped him over and down he went into the ground, head first. It was accidental, but it was illegal, and it looked ugly. Steve apologised twice to Plowman on the field. He was to face the judiciary on Tuesday night in Sydney.

The Broncos weren't too keen on losing their star centre to suspension. On the flight down to Sydney for the hearing at the ARL judiciary, Martin Burn QC, John Ribot and Steve sat working out their best defence. For an hour they anticipated the prosecution's case, developing a counter to each element of the argument. Steve committed everything to memory. It would be alright. If he kept to the strategy, there had to be a fair chance of getting off.

Steve faced the three judges. It was all very formal. 'You're in there. You're in your best clobber. You feel like a criminal,' Steve says. 'You're in there for an incident on a footy field and you feel like you're in a proper court of law.'

Steve sat and listened. He was shown a video of the incident. When he was asked, 'What have you got to say, Steve?', he looked straight at the panel. 'Watching that, I feel sick,' he admitted. That was it. He was suspended for two weeks. 'I just blew it there and then,' he remembers. 'I virtually told them how bad it looked.'

He returned for the Broncos–Easts match, and, as was often the case when returning from a break, he played brilliantly, scoring three tries in the 44–12 win.

His good form continued. A month later the Broncos played Balmain at Optus Oval in Melbourne. Steve had another one of those days out. He scored four tries himself as the Broncos flogged the Tigers 36–14.

Why did this happen from time to time? Why were there days when he played so brilliantly? Steve can't explain it:

I'm a Carlton supporter so I was quite rapt to be playing at their home ground. It was one of those days where I just enjoyed myself. Everything went right. I felt like I could run at a hundred miles an hour. I was very much a 'feeler' player. That day I felt magnificent. It was hard to work out why. Wayne would always be looking for a pattern. And you're trying to find out what caused it yourself; what you did before the match maybe. But I found these days came when I didn't think too much. If I did too much thinking or I had too much going on in my head beforehand, I might as well not run out there.

Steve was certainly different – and interesting. People wanted to know more about him. In the profiles being penned, he was being compared to the greats. Ian Heads, in the *Sydney Morning Herald*, suggested he was on the verge of becoming 'one of the most thrilling centres the game has ever seen', comparing him to the 'supremely gifted Australian centres' of the generations: Dally Messenger, Herb Gilbert, Dave Brown, Reg Gasnier, Bob Fulton, Steve Rogers, Mick Cronin and Mal Meninga. Asked his opinion of Renouf, Steve Rogers said: 'He'd be the first picked in my side . . . He's got everything it takes – acceleration, long-range speed and he sure can hit a hole.'

In the *Big League Magazine* Reg Gasnier was quoted as saying: 'He's the best in the game. [He's] got all the attributes – the pace, the step . . . he just goes like a bullet. No one gets near him at the moment . . . His defence is spot on. He's just a super all-round player.'

In the same article Chris Johns said: 'I'm amazed at him at least once a game. The way he can make space for himself is something else.'

The profiles gave a hint at what Steve was like, but there was never the definitive piece. He was featured in Matthew Fynes-Clinton's article in *Inside Sport*, where Wayne Bennett was quoted as saying, 'One of the great sights in sport has been to see Steve Renouf come through a gap . . . just the flow and rhythm. Big Mal's about to retire and I think Steve's going to be the dominant centre in Australian Rugby League for a long time. A coach couldn't give him what he's got there. Anything he can do with a football, I couldn't coach him in.'

In *Who Weekly* and *New Idea* he was portrayed as the family man. Rugby league publications gave footballing insights. He was the 'prince of centres', the 'Rolls Royce'. He was 'magic'. We learnt that his favourite item of clothing was a pair of old Rugger shorts, that his favourite meal was sausages and onion gravy, that he liked Clint Eastwood and AC/DC, that he was afraid of the dark (still).

We learnt something of his past. Wayne Smith described him as 'Murgon's Magic Man'. In becoming the toast of Murgon, Smith said Steve was helping to heal the divisions in the community following the death of Dermot Tiernan. 'He is doing this by being a local Aboriginal, born and bred, working hard to make the most of his talents,' Smith wrote. 'He has not sought to become a spokesman for his people . . . Renouf is comfortable playing the role model but he has turned it into a non-speaking part.' He quoted Steve: 'I like to think I'm doing the right thing by Aboriginal people just by setting an example. Hopefully I can show Aboriginal youngsters what can be achieved.'

It wasn't just the newspapers of the News Ltd stable that were interested in Steve. Peter FitzSimons produced an article for the *Sydney Morning Herald*, a Fairfax paper, headed 'Bucko the Bronco: doing it his way', in which he noted that Steve had 'no apparent ego yet' nor was he preoccupied with football. 'I don't like watching footy on television so the only games I see are the ones I play in,' Steve confessed to the former Australian rugby player. FitzSimons certainly captured Steve's laid-back nature.

There were even more family photos after their second child, William Charles Renouf, was born in May. Then Steve and Lis knew they were alive: two kids under eighteen months. And, as Lis said in one TV interview, she still wanted six.

In the lead-up to the first State of Origin match that year, Steve was again the focus of attention. 'Renouf in the hot seat,' read the *Courier-Mail* headline. Gene Miles claimed: '[Steve Renouf] is probably under more pressure than any player on the field . . . Steve's form in club football has been so exceptional a lot of people are looking at him and expecting him to make the same impact in State of Origin.' Paul Malone reported: 'Renouf sagged at the knees in mock fatigue and nerves when reminded yesterday of the expectations on him.' It may not have been mock nerves. At that stage he had never completed a full State of Origin match and was just looking to play all three in the series. He was, as always, keen to team up with Mal Meninga in the centres.

In the first match at the Sydney Football Stadium, New South Wales came out firing. Steve reckons the Maroons really struggled and were 'shot ducks' midway through the second half. The Blues were confident out on the paddock and had a bit to say. But Queensland clawed their way back from 12–4 down. Steve made a break which resulted in a Willie Carne four-pointer. Meninga converted: 12–10. They hadn't been near it all night but with two minutes to go they were alive. In possession well inside their own territory, they had to take some risks. Wayne Bennett described the moment in his book *Don't Die with the Music in You*:

> Desperate yet controlled, Willie Carne knew his pass had to go over the top, and that he could throw it one-handed, on to Steve Renouf, whose juggling act with the ball we'd seen a thousand

times in training with the Broncos. With practice, there needs to be little or no thinking. Thinking with practice transforms to instinct. No way did Renouf have to think about catching that ball . . . Renouf – Hancock – Darren Smith, they all drew their respective men before what was the critical part, involving Langer, Meninga and Coyne. Mark Coyne had been involved way back at the play-the-ball where Meninga was the dummy-half and Langer the first receiver, and all they did was stay alive heading straight down field.

Langer to Meninga to Coyne. Coyne reached out as he was tackled to just get the ball down to score a try that will be remembered for a long time. Everyone ran to the corner. 'It was sensational,' Steve says. 'We were jumping around. They were shell-shocked. Blokes like Brad Mackay – he'd had great game, as always – couldn't believe it. They'd been pretty cocky in the first half.' Meninga converted. Queensland won 16–12 to go one up in the series.

Steve missed the second match through injury. The Blues won that game 14–0 in front of a monster crowd at the MCG. He returned for the decider at Lang Park but, despite scoring himself, Queensland lost the game 27–12. Yet again Steve felt unsatisfied by Origin football.

With the Origin series out of the way, the Broncos were again expected to finish the season strongly. They needed to, languishing as they were in ninth position on the ladder. There was a hint of complacency in the camp – and a distraction or two. There were whispers there could be changes in the organisation of the ARL competition.

After a string of good wins the Broncos finished fifth in the 1994 season and took on Manly in the first week of the finals. It was a tight contest in which the game was turned by a quintessential outball. Steve reckons it was a classic example of the move. 'We were inside our own half,' he recalls. 'There was a scrum with a short blind. But I stayed on that left side with Terry Hill marking me. Kevvy just gave me the nod and I said fair enough. I moved myself ever-so-slightly wider, with little fairy steps, until I had enough on [Hill]. I don't reckon he noticed. I still remember taking that ball and Terry Hill knew he was beaten. He put his head down. You can see little things in your peripheral vision and I just remember his body language. We'd caught him out.' Steve ran 80 metres to score.

But the win had its price. Steve had been involved in an awkward tackle on Manly winger Jack Elsegood. As Elsegood was on the ground Steve slid into him, catching him in the side with his knees, damaging Elsegood's ribs. Steve assured everyone it was an accident. The Sydney media assured everyone that Renouf deserved to be cited, which he eventually was. They reckoned he deserved four weeks suspension.

It was *the* issue of the second finals' week and heightened the rift that was developing between the Broncos and Sydney. Despite the controversy, Steve was photographed smiling at training, his nonchalance and sense of perspective most healthy in the melodrama. Bennett didn't make a fuss. He just asked Steve about the tackle. When Steve replied, 'I didn't mean to hurt him,' that was good enough for the coach. There was no malice in Steve on the footy field.

Journalists milked the story for all it was worth. As Steve left for Sydney, plenty of Queenslanders thought the NSW conspiracy had him guilty already. For their money, he'd been tried by the media and was unlikely to get a fair hearing.

Given Steve's performance at the judiciary earlier in the year, the Broncos weren't going to trust him with just one barrister. This time, as well as Martin Burn QC, Ian Callinan QC, one of Queensland's leading silks, was brought in on the case.

At that time, Mr Callinan was acting for the Criminal Justice Commission in the Court of Appeal where he was arguing for the CJC's power to keep information confidential. Most punters couldn't have given a rat's about the CJC. As they tucked into their rissoles and mash, they knew the Renouf case was of far greater public importance and Mr Callinan QC had a responsibility to act on behalf of the state of Queensland. The Broncos needed Steve Renouf. Queensland needed Steve Renouf. Besides, they believed that Pearl was innocent.

Ian Callinan was at his eloquent best. Steve kept comparatively quiet, using the word 'accidental' wherever he could – and the case was dismissed. He was free to play against Norths.

At the time the decision was handed down, Wayne Bennett was driving with his son Justin. They were listening to 'Bob the Kelpie', one of Justin's favourite songs, over and over, until Wayne convinced Justin to put the radio on for the 9 o'clock news. They heard that Steve had been cleared. From that moment 'Bob the Kelpie' became one of Wayne's favourite songs as well.

That weekend, however, the Broncos could find no magic. In one of the most frustrating games Steve reckons he ever played in, the Broncos were camped in Norths' half for the last quarter of the game but couldn't find a way to score a point. Then the Bears took the ball up the other end and Jason Taylor potted a field goal. There would be no third premiership.

Steve had had another excellent season, scoring twenty-three tries. He was still regarded as the most dangerous outside-back in the country. His peers concurred. In *Rugby League Week*'s Players' Poll, 70 per cent of NRL footballers voted Pearl the best centre in the competition. They voted him the most entertaining player, and the fourth best player overall.

Everyone knew Steve Renouf was an automatic selection for the 1994 Kangaroos tour. But this champion young footballer didn't want to go. It may have appeared that he didn't want to play. He did. It was just that other things were more important to him. Like family.

Other things were more important. He had serious doubts about being away from home for a ten-week tour, away from Lis and Sam, and away from Billy, who was just four and a half months old and had been unwell throughout September.

He felt uncomfortable and unsettled about it. Restless. Like it was the wrong thing to do. He wanted to find a way out. He approached Wayne Bennett and Kelvin Giles and asked them to help him come up with an excuse not to go. They were taken aback. Bennett thought Steve should go, even though he would have accepted Steve's decision either way.

Bennett remembers Steve being very worried and very coy about it all. He could tell how heart-wrenching it was for Steve to be away from his immediate family and his extended family and the places he knew as home. But he also believed that facing the challenge of the tour would be good for Steve as a person and as a player. 'It was a huge thing for him to overcome,' he recalls. 'But I was encouraging him to go.'

Steve took the advice of his mentor. He has mixed feelings about the tour. He enjoyed the experience of being in a country that he found at once similar to and vastly different from his own. He played well enough and the team was successful enough. The Australians won seventeen of their eighteen matches, and, after losing the first Test against Great Britain 8–4, they won the next two Tests easily. Steve especially loved the two weeks when Lis and Billy joined the touring party in England. Sam stayed at home with the grandparents Bishop.

After Lis and Billy returned to Australia, Steve and the Kangaroos continued to France where they thrashed the home side 74–0 in the only Test match. The long tour was over and

Steve was very keen to get home. Sam had just turned two when Lis brought him out to the airport to be reunited with his dad. What followed knocked Steve for six. 'Sam didn't recognise me,' he confides. 'While I was away he had gone through that change where he was able to recognise people. And I had missed that part of his development. That's exactly what I didn't want. I was shattered. He just didn't recognise me.'

It was a feeling he didn't want to experience again.

CHAPTER 10

Super League

THE BRONCOS HAD failed to win a third premiership in 1994, but there had been a few distractions. One was to take rugby league by the scruff of the neck.

The evening before the Illawarra game in Wollongong that year, Steve was having dinner with Alfie Langer and Chris Johns and some other players when into the hotel restaurant popped John Ribot. He had something on his mind. 'Ribes put up a bit of a hypothetical,' Steve remembers. He asked them what they would think if another competition was set up which offered the players much better money.

Ribot threw a few figures around. The amounts certainly made them sit up. 'The boys were all pumped,' Steve says. 'He was getting us on side. He was going around the table. This is what you'd be worth; this is what you'd be worth. They were good numbers. And obviously it was pretty attractive to everyone. But it was only hypothetical!'

Steve had no idea who was behind it all. No one was asking. They were all just spending the money – before they had it. Racehorses for Alf. Swimming pool for Kevvy. A nice house in the country for Pearl. Over the following months there were hushed conversations everywhere.

While the players were away on the Kangaroos tour there was a lot happening behind the scenes back in Australia. Changes, it seemed, were to be made to the structure of the top competition. A special league of ten or twelve clubs, administered by the ARL, was proposed. News Ltd hoped to be involved in some way. The company wanted to establish a relationship with the ARL which would give them the rights to broadcast the proposed competition on pay-TV, thereby taking Alf and Kevvy and Pearl into the lounge rooms of the world.

Kerry Packer wasn't impressed. He held the free-to-air rights until 2000, and he didn't fancy a competitor sniffing around. The Packer–Murdoch rivalry went back a long way. Both knew that a significant component of the sports-media business of the future lay in pay-TV. And Packer was not about to give Murdoch the inside running.

The competition was restructured for the 1995 season but not in the way the speculation had suggested. It was actually expanded. Four new teams were invited into the league. Kerry Packer took action to eliminate any chance of a Super League being set up. He insisted the twenty clubs who were to take part in the 1995 season each sign a loyalty agreement with the ARL. They all did, even the Broncos, despite the club's stormy relationship with the ARL. This agreement precluded clubs from joining a rival competition in the immediate future.

Talk of the breakaway competition, however, didn't go away. Steve didn't take much notice of what was happening. He was already on a very healthy contract until the end of 1995 and he knew he was in a strong position to renegotiate. Ribot's hypothetical was attractive but he and Lis were content. They were looking to buy a country property not long down the track, before the kids got too big. Somewhere on the outskirts of Brisbane where the kids would be able to run around, and Lis could keep a few animals. Steve was well and truly established as a professional footballer. He believed he was a footballer. He was in the happy position that the thing he loved to do was paying the bills.

The Broncos started the 1995 pre-season in fine form, winning the final of the Tooheys Cup against Cronulla 30–14 in Albury, on the Murray. It is a game Steve remembers, not for his on-field performance but for a conversation he had with the coach on the way to the game.

Steve and Wayne Bennett both hated flying in light planes and they found themselves sitting side by side up the back as they were buffeted all the way from Sydney to Albury. They got to talking and had a conversation which wandered all over the place. Steve was telling Wayne about his cousin who had a disability and how his aunt and uncle had always loved and cared for him, with dignity, with the assumption that his life was different but had its own meaning. Steve looked up to see Wayne with tears in his eyes.

Steve missed the first game of the new season. His toe had been caught awkwardly in the Albury final, and although there was no break there was damage to tendons and ligaments. He missed two weeks. The Broncos wanted him back but Steve knew the injury wasn't right. He would need a local anaesthetic in order to play. The pressure was on him. He was persuaded to play. He wasn't too happy, but he acknowledges that he was the one who made the final decision.

He moved well during the Broncos win against Illawarra at Steelers Stadium. But as soon as the anaesthetic wore off he was hobbling around and in a lot of pain. The news wasn't good and that week Steve had surgery to repair the ruptured ligaments in his foot. He would be out for three months.

While Steve lay on the operating table, the world of rugby league was in a spin. Not that Steve knew anything about it in the days that followed. Doped up on pain-killers, he was oblivious to all the activity.

That sort of thing always seemed to happen to Steve Renouf.

While Steve sat, foot-up, watching a *Wiggles* video with Sam, Alfie Langer and Willie Carne were at a house in the Brisbane suburb of Hamilton with Lachlan Murdoch and John Ribot. The young tycoon and his trusty sidekick were explaining that there was going to be a Super League, and that it was to be independent of the ARL. It would happen sooner rather than later, most likely the following year, 1996. News Ltd was set to challenge the legality of the ARL loyalty agreements in court. John Ribot had resigned from his position as CEO of the Broncos to become CEO of Super League and was therefore an employee of News Ltd. He had a lot of work to do. Super League needed players and it needed clubs and the Murdochs were happy to use the persuasive force of cash.

Alf sat there, beer in hand, listening. There would be a sign-on fee, and then an annual amount for three years. Alf looked at the figures. He'd hit the jackpot. He signed. Then Willie Carne signed. The following day all but a couple of Broncos signed at John Ribot's home. The Broncos would be a Super League club.

Steve was still laid up. No one had bothered to ring him, until finally, a few days later, John Ribot and one of the News Ltd accountants knocked on the door with an offer too good to refuse: a significant sign-on fee, and considerably more per year than his current contract. Steve signed then and there for three years.

After a day or so, Steve began wondering how he had fared in relation to the other players. It had never been the culture at the Broncos for players to compare the terms of their contracts, certainly not to talk about the dollar values. But, says Steve, Super League changed that. He recalls what happened:

I got wind of what the other guys had signed for, and I had signed for a lot less. So I got straight on the phone and said, 'Ribes, you got me.' He said, 'What do you mean, Bucko?' I said, 'You got me to sign for this [amount]', and I named a couple of players, which I wouldn't normally do, and I said, 'I think I'm worth at least what they're getting.' He said, 'Leave it with me.' He fixed it up. He increased the money and I wound up with a contract for *four* years (1996–99). I didn't even realise it was a four-year contract until a couple of years later when [the new Broncos CEO] Shane Edwards and I were looking through it and he said, 'Did you know this has an extra year on it?' We were both surprised.

Players had been offered very large amounts of money. The figures were reported inaccurately in the press. Steve says they were actually comparable to what the top players are on today nearly a decade later.

That weekend the Broncos played, and won, in Townsville. The media were only interested in the rumours about the breakaway competition. Anticipating an interrogation at the post-match press conference, the Super League bosses had written the script for Alf. He was instructed to say, 'Why would I sign a contract? I'm already under contract to an ARL club.' But he couldn't wipe the smirk from his face and as it came out he got the giggles. The room fell about laughing. The whole thing was a charade. The News Ltd journalists probably had a fair idea of what was going on anyway.

The ARL and especially Kerry Packer were not going to fall over. The race was on to sign clubs, established individual players, and potential young players. It was a good time to be in a

schoolboy rep side. Given that the pool of talent was comparatively small, the two warring camps felt they needed to pay good
money to ensure they had the future stars on-side. It was high-
risk investment.

The ARL went after the current stars as well, even those sus-
pected to have signed with Super League. A couple of days later
Steve and some of his Broncos mates were invited to talk to the
ARL officials. James Packer and Bobby Fulton had set up camp
in a private room at the Brisbane airport. They met with the
Broncos players one by one. Steve hobbled in and they buttered
him up. Here were the ARL representatives offering a man on
crutches an amount equivalent to the GDP of a small African
republic. Steve enjoyed being told how wonderful he was for a
quarter of an hour but he didn't sign anything.

It was a remarkable situation: a bloke who a few years before
had been a skinny little Murri kid running rings around them
in the dust of Murgon, now a pawn in the chess game of two
powerful corporate players – one of them a significant global
media magnate, the other one of the most powerful men in
Australia. The counter offers were substantial. Kevin Walters recalls
them being offered almost double what Super League had offered.

But the individual Broncos were probably unable to act even if
they had wanted to. The contracts they'd signed with Super
League appeared to be binding, although that would probably
have been sorted out in the courts later. Kevin Walters was
cautious because he had been warned by Super League. 'They
basically said,' Walters remembers, 'that if you signed with the
other mob it would be a breach of contract and you'd never play
again.'

Steve had heeded this warning. He went straight to Bennett
and told him what had happened, seeking his advice. When he
mentioned the sum he had been offered (which he actually

reduced a little bit), Bennett was amazed. 'Gee, they're after you if they're throwing that at you,' he replied.

Steve settled on Super League and was happy to do so. He was a Bronco, and the Broncos had signed. 'I signed on with Super League,' he explains, 'and, once I'd done that, Super League was my employer, and therefore my priority. I was committed to Super League, so whenever they asked me to do something I said yes. I was happy to show them loyalty – if there's any such thing in rugby league. It was like signing on at the Broncos.'

Immediately there was a massive marketing campaign in News Ltd newspapers. Steve was asked to appear in the ads. A week or so later a full-page photo of him appeared in the *Courier-Mail*, and underneath it were words attributed to Steve: 'If you think league is a fast game now, just wait for Super League.'

Steve flopped back in his lounge chair, watching it all unfold. Lis sat next to him. And the boys. Lis was just about to find out they had another baby on the way. They had cashed their sign-on cheque and after putting half away for the tax man they were still able to put a deposit on a 1930s timber home set on a ridge on an undulating piece of land in the Samford Valley. Lis could see it all coming together. It was picturesque, idyllic, perfect.

Looking back on it now, circumstances conspired to serve that group of players peculiarly well. Lis and Steve call it the era of 'funny money'. 'We were just lucky to be there at that time,' Lis acknowledges, 'although we weren't thinking that then – because we thought Super League was always going to be there. The promises were that this was going to be long-term. No one thought it was going to be so short.'

Not that the money changed Steve Renouf. ABC journalist Rod Kilner remembers putting together a news story on Steve that year. Not long before, his own son, Scot Kilner, a sports-loving 13-year-old, had been diagnosed with diabetes and was in the Caboolture Hospital. After Rod had taped the interview, he mentioned it to Steve, explaining how Scot had taken it pretty badly and was concerned it would encroach on his sporting life. Steve of his own accord went to visit Scot in hospital. The Kilners have never forgotten that.

The split altered rugby league for everyone – for the fans, the administrators, the media, the players. Although money and contracts were always part of professional rugby league, and an issue for players, they were always secondary issues somewhere in the background. Now off-field issues dominated football talk: politics, economics, legal issues, media issues. You couldn't take anything at face value. You first had to work out who was saying what, which camp they came from, and what agenda they were serving.

Fans watched as a game they had known and loved for years was changing in front of them and they were powerless to do anything about it. Many didn't feel right about what was happening.

Steve continued to sit out as his foot improved. He wouldn't have played Origin football that year anyway. No Super League players were picked for either side. Fatty Vautin's Queensland side scored a remarkable whitewash win in the Origin series.

Brisbane plugged away but they lacked fire-power without Pearl. 'Broncos in dire need of Renouf', a *Courier-Mail* headline announced. When he returned for Round 13 he was straight back into it, scoring two tries as the Broncos thrashed Parramatta 60–14. It was Darren Lockyer's first game. Coming off the bench, he made a huge impression. Kevin Walters was out injured for the game and had stayed in Brisbane. Some of the older players rang him from the dressing-room to sing him the club song. Then Chris Johns grabbed the phone: 'You're gone, Kevvy. Your career's over.' Walters had never heard of Darren Lockyer and didn't even recognise him from training.

Steve thought Lockyer had something special as soon as he saw him. He told Paul Malone in the *Courier-Mail* that the young player could be 'absolutely anything'. Kevvy was a creative genius, but he was no Carl Lewis. Lockyer had the ball skills – and the pace. With Walters and Lockyer in the same side, Steve was licking his chops.

A couple of weeks later Steve crossed twice in the 17–12 win against the Panthers at ANZ in yet another club match where his ability to break the line made the difference. And once through the defence he had the knack of scoring. In the last game of the home and away season, against Auckland at ANZ, he was unstoppable, notching up four tries before Wayne Bennett gave him a spell – halfway through the second half!

The Broncos were coming into September in good nick, but their poor run in finals continued, out in straight sets to Canberra 12–8 and the eventual premiers, the Bulldogs, 24–10. Injuries and a couple of dubious decisions didn't help things, but the performances were mediocre.

Often when the Broncos were in a slump there would be a crisis meeting at which the players would be addressed by the directors of the club and Wayne Bennett. It was a response to a sense of complacency which had crept in after the successful years of 1992–93; as if the boys had lost the hunger. Some players took it all very seriously, others laughed off yet another meeting. Steve reckons there were times when the group weren't as switched on as they should have been, and that they just took it for granted the wins would come. There was always the next match, the next season.

With football over, the Renoufs moved into the house in Samford. Lis had plans to renovate: walls out, verandahs extended, and a garden. It was all ahead of them, and they were looking forward to settling down and enjoying life as a family.

That summer things were still very much up in the air. News Ltd brought an action in the Federal Court against the ARL, testing the legality of the loyalty agreements. The hearing had started before Justice Burchett in the week after the Grand Final. The Broncos players clung to their contracts with News Ltd, assuming that they were binding, and that they would be paid for the duration of them. It seemed to be in black and white. But no one really knew. They could be reassured all they liked but there was still an uneasiness, particularly about what was going to happen to the game in 1996. Steve was, after all, a rugby league *player*. It's what he loved. Being out there, with the best.

It was a matter of waiting and waiting. Rugby league was in a state of disarray. There was no pre-season competition. Players prepared for a premiership season, the structure of which hadn't been decided. It all depended on Justice Burchett. Finally on February 23 he handed down his decision – in favour of the ARL. There would be no Super League. Kerry Packer and Ken Arthurson had won the day.

Rupert Murdoch immediately expressed his intention to appeal the decision. That appeal would be heard at the end of the 1996 season.

The players were still in limbo. The 1996 season proved to be one of the flattest. The Broncos, along with the other Super League clubs, forfeited their first-round match. The fans were restless. Attendances were down at Broncos matches. There were arguments in pubs about what was happening to the code. Money's buggerin' it up. Sip. In my day we played for nothin'. Sip. For the love of the jumper. Sip. Sip. I'm not interested anymore. Sip. Give me one of those meat tray tickets. Sip. Who's it for? Sip. Beenleigh juniors? Sip. What do you mean you haven't got enough money for jumpers?

Family Renouf just went about living. There may not have

been a lot of joy in football, but there was plenty of joy at the Mater Hospital where Lis presented Steve with a beautiful daughter, Sunita Grace. Sunny was named after an Indian girl, Suneetha, whom the Bishops had sponsored through World Vision. The new baby made three. Lis still thought, 'Six'. Steve thought, 'Really?'

The family would get back to Murgon when they could, staying with the Bishop grandparents and visiting Palmer Street. They'd usually catch up with Paul and Colleen. One afternoon Paul and Steve were out in the paddock chasing cattle and Bish wanted to talk football – to get the real story. He was keen to know what was going on and where all this Super League stuff was leading. They talked about the money involved. Bish asked whether the newspaper numbers were accurate. Most of them weren't. So Steve told him what he was being paid. 'I mentioned a big number to him,' Steve remembers. 'Bish said, "Is that for the four years?" I said, "No. Per year." Bish said, "Faaark". He had no idea.'

Steve felt a strong obligation to his employer. He continued to do what was asked of him. Sometimes it was quite demanding. He wasn't the type who'd say no to an autograph – or anything he was asked to do, really. Every second week he was on the front page of the *Courier-Mail* scoring another try. And the other weeks it would be something to do with work or his family. He was constantly in public view. There were times when, on a Monday or Tuesday, he wouldn't go to the shops because he knew it would take ages just to buy a few groceries. It could be wearing and there were occasional moments when he felt burdened by all of it, and by the situation of not knowing what the future really held.

Another time, visiting Murgon, Steve was a bit down about what was happening. Paul Bishop remembers it well. Usually

Steve was like his father, Old Charlie: happy and making the most of things. He was never one to complain, or give voice to his upset. But he said to Bish, 'Mate, football owns me.'

As much as he appreciated that life with the Broncos had given him a lot, there were times when he felt a little lost. When he went home to Murgon he was reminded of the inherent tension in his life. In Brisbane football wasn't only football. It was all of the things around football. While football had been primarily fun in Murgon, it could feel like a relentless grind in Brisbane.

The Broncos won eight games in a row after the first-round forfeit. Broncos players were eligible for selection in the State of Origin teams and Steve played in all three matches. New South Wales reversed their fortunes of the previous year, winning the series 3–0. Steve scored from a Langer bomb in the second match but he still didn't feel he had made much of a contribution at that level. He couldn't get into the games, and he still never felt good going into them.

The 1996 season conformed to the pattern of previous years: a solid start for the club, a struggle during the Origin period, and then a storming finish to the home-and-away season which had people thinking the Broncos were the team to beat. But the finals hoodoo continued and again the Broncos were out after two weeks, losing 21–16 to Norths and then 22–16 to Cronulla.

Manly won the premiership, but for the Broncos players all interest was in the result of Rupert Murdoch's appeal against the earlier Burchett decision. Steve and Lis had spent the season in a state of apprehension and they were genuinely worried about what might happen if the court threw out the appeal.

Steve wasn't leaving things completely to chance. Sydney City (an ARL club) had shown interest in him again and he met with their representative, Nick Polites, in a suite at a Brisbane hotel. The official was willing to do whatever it took to lure Steve across, before the decision was handed down. He offered more than Steve's Super League deal, and eventually just said, 'What do you want?' Steve was tempted. He had always had a soft spot for Easts, having barracked for them as a kid. If football is your livelihood, there are reasons to go where the best rewards are. But those rewards are not necessarily measured in dollars and cents. Steve didn't sign.

Knowing that they would either be very happy and relieved or very unhappy and concerned, the Renoufs booked a holiday on Lindeman Island for the week following the decision. They would either celebrate or drown their sorrows.

The Super League bosses wanted some of the Broncos players to be at the Federal Court for the handing down of the decision. Steve was flown to Sydney. On October 4 the court upheld the appeal. 'League of their own,' the *Courier-Mail* headline declared. 'Stunning court victory by News', 'A whole new ball game'. News Ltd was free to get the rival competition up and running. So Steve and Lis and baby Sunny went off to Lindeman relieved and very relaxed.

Times were a-changing.

In any community, division causes upset, and the rugby league community was divided in 1997. There were two competitions: the traditional ARL competition, and the Super League competition with teams dotted all around the country from Perth to Adelaide, Townsville to Canberra.

Brisbane had an extremely talented back line, and with the modified Super League rules which gave teams plenty of room to move, they played some open football. High scores were common. Darren Lockyer had established himself at full-back and, at just 20 years old, had a magnificent season.

The Broncos had also recruited Anthony 'Choc' Mundine, a light-footed, quick and constructive five-eighth by nature. But he was never going to displace Kevin Walters, so he played in the centres with Steve. The two highly talented Aboriginal men had very different personalities. Anthony was brash and cocky, and outspoken. Steve didn't say much at all.

Mundine struggled with injury during the season, playing only half of the games. When it became obvious he was not going to get the opportunities he'd hoped for, he returned to St George the following year. The Broncos players got on well with Choc. They wished him every success, and when he left football to take up boxing in 2000 quite a few of them flew to Sydney for his first fight.

The Broncos dominated the season. Steve had his ups and downs. The Super League equivalent of State of Origin was a Tri-series involving Queensland, New South Wales and New Zealand. The Maroons lost 38–10 to New South Wales in a match in which Steve had his jaw broken again. There were always injuries. When he returned later in the year, he helped Brisbane finish well clear at the top of the table. Lockyer was outstanding and he and Steve and Kevvy built up quite a relationship on the field. Steve reckons Lockyer was the best player in both competitions in 1997.

There was a lot happening off the field still and much speculation about the future of rugby league. The Broncos players were effectively staff of News Ltd, and that brought them into the News Ltd world. The company knew how to throw a good party and Steve was often invited. 'They laid it on,' Steve says. 'But I wasn't one to go looking for the celebs. If they were around I didn't notice.'

One night he did wind up at a Balmain pub where Russell Crowe's band was playing inside. But Steve was at a table outside singing 'American Pie' with Tom Cruise and Nicole Kidman. That these people were famous was of no consequence to Steve. That he found them to be good company was.

Fans felt a hollowness in rugby league that year. It was as if deep down people knew that commercial concerns had become the reason football was played – that football was serving a different master. There was also the simple practicality that the best weren't playing against the best.

The flow of the Super League season was also interrupted by the World Club Challenge, which involved club teams from the major rugby league countries. Some Australian clubs travelled to England, some English clubs to Australia. The games tended to be uninspiring, and often one-sided. The Broncos remained in Australia, winning one match against Halifax 76–0 without getting out of a canter.

Even the players felt that the rift had sapped the life out of rugby league. ARL and Super League teams would bump into each other in airports and, Steve remembers, 'Everyone was just saying the same thing: "I just wish this could be sorted out." We couldn't wait to get back together. There was no tension whatsoever between the players.'

With all of these distractions it took quite a bit to keep the players thinking about football. 'There was that much going on in our heads,' Steve recalls. 'Wayne's biggest fear was that we were worrying about all of that and not worrying about footy. He had plenty to say. He talked about it constantly. Give Wayne credit: he got our minds on track. We had a huge year.'

Brisbane and Cronulla, the two best teams in the Super League competition, played off in the Grand Final, the first ever held at night. In front of nearly 60,000 fans at ANZ Stadium, the Broncos dominated the match, taking the premiership 26–8. It was a comprehensive win. They had clearly been the best side all season and they had won the premiership. But, as happy as the fans were, there wasn't the same public acclamation as there had been for the back-to-back premierships.

Steve was outstanding. He scored the first three of the four Bronco tries, and was instrumental in the Broncos' impressive defensive effort. Peter Sterling regarded it as one of Steve's best all-round games.

Steve's third try was particularly satisfying for him. It came after a move down the left. Kevvy shot a bullet-pass to Lockyer who, with precise timing, turned it back inside to Pearl. Pearl whizzed through a little hole. Over for the try. If there is such a thing as perfection in sport this understated move approached it. The ball was too quick. Steve was too quick. Every muscle moved just as it needed to, in a fluid motion of speed and evasion. There was no conscious effort or thought, just movement.

Steve was not one to celebrate his tries. He always felt great on the inside, but he didn't show much on the outside. For once he let loose. It was his way of saying to two footballers, Kevvy and Locky, that he respected them. He knew that they all knew what it had taken to do what they'd just done. Steve jumped into Kevvy's arms, and Kevvy's face told the story: 'Is Pearl OK?' And then Steve found Locky. That was an embrace of talent.

Sport can give you transcendent moments like this.

CHAPTER 11

A Footballer's Life

YET AGAIN THERE was uncertainty for Steve Renouf and his young family. It seemed that the unhappy world of rugby league was on a path of self-destruction. The two hungry organisations had an idea that, if there wasn't some sort of compromise, both might lose substantially.

So there was relief in the Renouf household when that compromise was reached. There would be a unified competition. The 1998 season was one of the most important in rugby league. The game had a core of fans who would always stay with it, but the split had disillusioned many supporters. In Brisbane, the rise of the Brisbane Bears and then their merger with Fitzroy to become the Brisbane Lions meant that the club was attracting patrons and sponsors. Rugby league needed a stellar season to restore people's faith in the code.

It got one, and while internal problems saw the Brisbane Lions finish at the bottom of the ladder, the Brisbane Broncos continued where they'd left off in the Super League. They won their first five matches and played a brand of entertaining football which thrilled the crowds. There was a sense that the globe was back on its axis and spinning as it was meant to.

Steve was 27 at the start of the season: an experienced pro. Those tough days, when he had fought with himself to become the player the Broncos expected him to be, were in some ways a long way off. But, like anyone who has their performance assessed weekly by a media in need of a story – and a hyper-critical public – Steve sometimes felt the pressure. Lis was unfailing in her encouragement of him. Sometimes he drove her crazy with his carefree attitude, but she loved him just the same.

Steve also loved the company of his team-mates. They had grown very close over nearly a decade together. Alf and Kevvy made him laugh. He was like the little sister in a family of ratbag brothers: quiet and on the edge looking in but happy to be with them. Their sense of fun kept them all sane in the craziness of the incessant demands of a football week.

Steve had grown into his role. He was an established player, a senior player. He believed he was in the right place. 'I was happy,' he reflects. 'That was my home. I was comfortable with the people around me. I was comfortable with the coach. I could be the most creative in club footy.'

He loved two places in particular: ANZ Stadium where he played so many terrific games and scored so many tries, and sitting in front of his locker at Fulcher Road.

He had learnt to live within the weekly rhythm of football life; the rhythm of preparation, play and review. The bigger picture of finals and possible premierships is always there, but footballers really do take it one week at a time.

The routine of the week didn't change much over the years. Monday was a quiet day. Steve would be deflated after the week-end's match. Even for a normal club game there is a build-up to a match, a slow process where players are readied to give of themselves on the footy field, a process which builds to the crescendo that is the hour and a half of the game. Most matches have a phenomenal intensity and players give their all. Win or lose, matches are draining: physically, mentally, emotionally, spiritually.

So Monday was often a let-down day. Sometimes Steve would read the *Courier-Mail*'s coverage of the football. Sometimes not. He never videotaped the games to watch again. He knew he'd see some of the action at the team meeting during the week. The Broncos would meet for a swim and a stretch at Jindalee. There were usually a couple of players looking for the Beroccas. The mood of the group varied according to the weekend's perform-ance. Later that day they'd meet again for Monday Club, where they would get their win bonus and then try and avoid Alf.

Tuesday morning was gym work, followed by a light session of ball work. And then came the team meeting at which the week-end's performance was reviewed. Blokes sat in the same seat year in year out. Bennett would give his summation, using the video to highlight the good and the bad. The team never watched the whole game. Players were reminded of team rules and strategies, and if they were having trouble sticking to them fines would be instituted for the following week.

After one match in which it seemed every Bronco and his dog wanted to roost the football downfield, Bennett was furious. New team rule: only the set-kickers can kick *at any time*. No exceptions. There would be a $300 fine if anyone else's foot touched the ball. The following week in the match against Penrith Steve found himself in a situation where, instinctively, he grub-bered through for Willie Carne. 'I wasn't even thinking,' Steve says. 'Of course, Willie scored off it.' It was a clever option and a brilliant try. 'Now Benny had a problem,' Steve recalls. 'I was just waitin' and waitin'. Everyone was havin' a go. We got to the team meeting – I skipped the fine.'

Steve was the sort of player who could make the notion of team rules appear ridiculous. Not that he was wilfully challenging them, or the coach's authority. He just did things on the footy field that even he felt he had no control over. He often wondered, 'Where did that come from?'

More often than not, though, Steve's gift wasn't a problem for Bennett, and Bennett delighted in acknowledging it. 'Wayne always talked about the special talent Aboriginal players have,' Steve says. 'We'd be sitting in a team meeting watching the video and I might have been involved or scored a try and he'd just say, "I can't coach that". That was very flattering.'

The praise made Steve feel good, but he felt a deeper satisfaction than that. It was the affirmation of his heritage. Not that he showed it. He would acknowledge the compliment but sit there quietly, looking a little coy about it all.

Glen Lazarus and Kevvy Walters were the talkers, the theorists, the speculators. After a good performance the mood was happy and light. After a shocker it was sombre. Bennett could sense when the boys were contrite. He could tell when they cared. And when they didn't, he let them know.

At some point during the meeting there was a transition from reflection to preparation for the weekend coming. From that moment on, the previous game was forgotten. This had to be genuine. Bennett would talk about opposition strategies, and the strengths and weaknesses of individual opponents. He would initiate the ideas for the Broncos' strategy as well.

After the meeting there would be a traditional Tuesday afternoon training, the length of which depended entirely on the boys' ability to complete the tasks to the satisfaction of the coach. Some sessions would go on and on. Alf and Kevvy would crack, talking out of the corner of their mouths in some remote Ipswich dialect, making comments like, 'Red Rooster shuts at

10', just loud enough for the coach to hear. Bennett would shoot back, 'Boys, I got all night. I'm in no hurry to go anywhere. You get it right, you can go.'

By the late 1990s most of the team weren't training to win a spot on the team, and often it was difficult to keep the motivation and the concentration up. They were established, ten-year players – some of the finest in the world. They were given a simple incentive, one which appeals to all professional sportsmen caught in the demands of an ongoing routine: if the group trained well on Tuesday night, there was a good chance they'd be given Wednesday off. They always had Friday off. But an extra day off was treasured.

On Tuesday night the weekend's team was selected, enabling the side to train in that combination for the remainder of the week. If there was training on Wednesday, it was a light ball-work session.

Thursday was busy: gym first, followed by ball-work, and then lunch. The boys could go where they liked for lunch and Steve would occasionally duck down to KFC on Kelvin Grove Road. He'd find himself in a queue of shiny vehicles driven by Broncos players. Then they'd return to the club for a light fitness workout.

On Friday Steve could be involved in anything from jobs around the house to a game of golf. Often during the week there were hospital visits and appearances for charities, at community organisations and at schools. Some players might be required at a sponsor's function. Steve might even get to go to work at Australia Post (although Andrew Johns remembers running into an Australia Post employee in a pub in Spring Hill who reckoned he hadn't seen Steve in four years).

Compared with the requirements of Steve's work in the real world today (with the Queensland Government's Department of Sport and Recreation) being a Bronco wasn't actually too taxing on one's time. The difficulty came in remaining focused and switched on – and keeping out of the medical room.

If the game was on Sunday, the team would have a 45-minute run at Fulcher Road on Saturday morning, followed by a shower and a barbecue breakfast. Steve always enjoyed those mornings, as they signified the end of the training week, and he could look forward to the game. If they were playing away, they'd catch a flight at around 2 pm, and then get to the hotel, take it easy, and have dinner. They might watch a movie, or the Saturday game on TV, or just sit around and chat. There was always a bit of waiting around in the morning. Maybe a walk. A hit of tennis. And then came the game.

Virtually every second week the Broncos played in Brisbane. Steve would start his match day with his normal breakfast of cereal and toast. And then would begin the long wait. In the early years he just sat around, taking it easy, but later on he needed to occupy the time, so it might be more jobs around the house, or doing something with the kids. He'd have a light early lunch: a sandwich and some fruit. Food wasn't a concern for him at all, as it can be for some footballers who can't have anything in their stomachs when they play.

(Sometimes it was hard not to eat. One night at Shark Park Steve got off the team bus with John Plath and they were overwhelmed by the smell of the food, especially the pies. Steve said to Plathy, 'I gotta get one of them.' So the two top-class footballers wolfed down a pie each an hour before the first whistle.)

Suddenly it would be time to go to ANZ Stadium and Steve would race around looking for his gear. 'I was always pretty shabby with that stuff,' he says, laughing. 'It was always at the last minute. Me yelling out to Lis, "Where are my socks?"' He never cleaned his boots, other than to wipe a bit of the mud off them.

Sometimes they'd be wet and smelly from the week before. Steve used to think, 'What the heck, it's only a game of footy.'

Steve had a lot of foot injuries during his career and it was hard to find boots that he was comfortable in. He tried to have some custom-made, with the appropriate markings stuck onto them, but the sponsor wouldn't allow it. Steve was also often chipped by the team manager for not wearing the right running shoes to training. But it was always only a warning, never a fine.

When his children were younger, a day at the football took a lot of organising. Keeping three kids happy was a lot for one mum, especially when Lis wanted to watch Steve, so often the kids would stay at home with a babysitter. As Steve and Lis drove to ANZ Stadium, Steve reckons he was always slightly 'on edge'. Lis prefers to describe him as 'a bit grumpy'.

They'd park the car and sit in the grandstand to watch a few minutes of the Reserve Grade game. Just before half-time Steve would head down to the dressing sheds. As he was about to leave he'd kiss Lis's cheek. She would hold up a number of fingers to indicate how many tries she wanted him to give her. She'd smile and nod. And Steve would be a little embarrassed. It was their ritual.

Steve liked to get to the sheds early so he didn't have to wait to be strapped. He'd throw his bag in the spot under his peg (there were no lockers). He'd sit for a minute, enjoying that hollow echo that half-empty dressing rooms have. Then he'd have his ankles taped and get in line for a rub. He liked oil and a bit of heat. The masseur would give him a ten-minute work-over. Sometimes he'd even nod off for a few minutes. He'd wake up disorientated and then realise where he was and think, 'Jeez, I've got to play a game of football'.

In Sydney one of the masseurs was old Frankie. Frankie had rubbed footballers for years. He'd give the boys a rub the night before at the hotel and then before the game the next day. He had a thousand stories about the old days. But he was more famous for the callus or broken nail he had which Steve remembers 'would scratch the crap out of you'. Alf and Kevvy and Steve used to talk about it, but no one ever mentioned it to him.

There was no music in the ANZ rooms. Very few, if any, players wore headphones. Steve would sit there pulling on his socks and boots. The team manager, Brian 'Noosy' McGrath, would give Steve his jumper. Wayne Bennett would appear but he wouldn't impose his presence at all. He'd say g'day here and there and have a bit of a chat with a few players. There'd be a few blokes kicking footballs to themselves, or passing to each other.

Bennett would be reading the signals. Steve reckons he was a master at detecting how well the boys had prepared, and were preparing; what their focus was like. He might convey a specific instruction privately to one of the players. It was all very low-key. Bennett knew it was a rare day when his men didn't have pride in their performance. He knew what football meant to them individually, and collectively as the Broncos. He trusted them.

The boys would then be taken outside for a solid stretching session. The game wasn't far away now. Steve tried not to think too much, but he had a special football feeling, quite difficult to describe. He felt a certain fear. Not the absence of courage. Far from it, because football demands you muster all of the courage in you. It was more a sense of respect. Respect for what might happen on the field. Respect for the other players who he knew were feeling the same way. Respect for what it takes to be at your best.

Rugby league is a tantalising game. It invites you to show what skill you have, but in an environment of constant physical threat. It is about overcoming the knowledge of pain. If you are an attacking player like Steve, it's about your forwards putting themselves on the line to batter the opposition into submission so the creative players can perform their magic.

Steve dealt with his feelings privately. He wasn't one to pump himself up by chesting team-mates or giving those loud guttural roars which help some players find their primitive selves. He was just hoping he'd feel good, because then he knew he'd be in for a good game. The problem was that, even after ten years, he couldn't work out where that feeling came from, or what it was that made Steve Renouf feel good.

We live in a culture that seeks to observe and explain things so we can reproduce them. Steve didn't need to explain the feeling. He recognised it when it happened – and enjoyed it. Celebrated it.

In the half hour before the match, these players made their final preparations. Blokes sprang up and down. Blokes smacked their hands into footballs. Blokes bumped into each other. Blokes yelled encouragement. Then, in the last moments before they left the dressing room, Wayne Bennett would address the players. Maybe five minutes of calm, even gentle, words. 'He'd talk,' Steve explains. 'And then he'd give you a break. He'd say, "Have a think for a few moments". And everyone would just go quiet. It was like a prayer. Everyone just had a think.'

After a few final words from Bennett the boys were ready. They'd line up as they left the sheds. Alf first. Then Kevvy. Then Steve. Always in that order. If you watch the tapes of these games, you'll see these three small footballers, who look like they could be playing for the Kickatinalong Primary School.

It was a long walk to the field at the ANZ Stadium: underneath the grandstand, then right and up and over the athletics track, out of the shadows and into the light of day. Steve loved that first cheer that went up. That acknowledgment from the crowd that these were *their* boys. Once he hit the turf, he'd do a short sprint and wind up near Mick Hancock and they'd hit their hands together the way players do when they're interchanged.

Kevvy was always yelling footy stuff, like, 'C'arn, fellas.' And the boys would get ready for the kick-off. The ref would blow his whistle and it was on again.

It often took Steve a long time to get into the game, to even touch the ball, despite the best efforts of Alf and Kevvy. 'Sometimes,' Kevvy reckons, 'he was happier having a chat with the people in the first row of the crowd.' But once he got into the game, things happened. He was always the performer, the archetypal strike player, although by the time he had become a senior player he was more conscious of his responsibilities. The actual result mattered much more to him than it had earlier in his career.

He'd also learnt the tricks of the trade: he and Alf were permanently off-side out in the backs. Steve would say, 'Piss off, Alf, you're getting me in trouble.' Alf reckons that in all those years Steve never learnt how to pass from dummy half, and that he was the slowest distributor in the history of the game.

At half-time the team would walk off together and they'd all sit in their spots. Alf would be mumbling. Kevvy wouldn't shut up. Other blokes would be yelling things, but again, Steve reckons, it was reasonably calm, even when the team was in trouble. Bennett was not one to rant and rave, although he did have his moments. If chaos reigned, Bennett would quickly get things back in order. 'Sometimes Benny would come in and tell us to shut up,' Steve says. 'Because what was being said wasn't always constructive stuff. He'd talk. It was a matter of finding a single path. In life there are many paths, but in football you need a common path . . . Benny is a fantastic judge. He could read a game. He'd have a few things to work on straightaway. Very specific. And very clear.'

Steve always did a blood test at half-time. His sugar level was unlikely to be high, and if it was he didn't need to act because he was burning it up on the field. If it was low, he needed to eat something. But throughout his career his diabetes didn't cause him any problems on the football field.

The players would run back on for the second half, and the battle would resume. Once Steve got into the game he felt at home. He loved it. Chris Johns says, 'Steve didn't play to win premierships. He played to enjoy himself.' His team-mates agree about Steve's motivation, but even Steve would not dispute that a win was better than a loss. Steve was not a selfish player. He just had a different attitude to football generally, and there was enough compromise from Steve and from Wayne Bennett to enable us to see what Steve was able to do on a footy field.

When the final hooter sounded, Steve always shook hands with his opponents. He respected them, and they respected him. Rarely was there any ill-feeling. There was usually a sense of camaraderie among them; they understood what they had just been through, irrespective of the result, and friendships could be reconstituted after that final whistle.

There might be a media interview while walking off. Cameras flashing. Blokes ripping tape off themselves. A wave to the crowd. Hands clapping above heads to thank the fans for their support. And then back underneath, and away into the sheds.

Steve loved plonking down at his spot. The fellas would file in, happy if they'd had a win. Then Noosy McGrath would lead them in the team song:

Weeeellll . . .
The Broncos are our name
Through the north we won our fame
Being handy with the ball

And we drove the Blues insane
And we put on a move
And we scored a certain try
So sing out our alibi.

You didn't know, we had to beat yuh
And we're so sorry my friends
You didn't know we had to beat yuh
And we'll never ever do it again
Bullshit.

'That celebration was important to me,' says Steve.

A winning dressing room is a great place to be. Bodies are exhausted. Some need patching up. But everyone is more than just ordinary-happy. They have a deeper satisfaction. There'd be laughter as they sat around. 'How was that pass from Kevvy? What about Gee Gee's hit?' There'd be the 'Chhhhh' of beers being cracked, and food was there for those who wanted it.

Then into the showers. Water has amazing powers of rejuvenation, and spirits were always high in the showers after a win. Then into the after-match kit, throw everything in the bag, throw the bag over the shoulder, and go through the door that takes you back into the real world.

Invariably there would be fans waiting to receive their heroes, and they'd offer a few words of congratulation: 'Well done, Pearl.' And the youngsters would be after autographs. Steve would always spend time signing his name, especially in the basketball gym under the stand.

Then he'd find Lis. It was always great to see her. She was always proud of him, whatever happened, and always had the right words: quiet celebration after a good performance, quiet comfort at times of defeat or injury.

They would drive to the club where everyone would gather

for a post-match function, which included a few words from Billy J. Smith and a presentation or two. After dinner at the club, they'd head home to Samford by about 9.30. It was always a long and tiring day, usually rewarding and occasionally uplifting. But they were always glad to get home to the kids.

That weekly routine had gone on for years. And Steve was comfortable with it. He was very much at home at the Broncos.

It was his place.

The club was well-positioned coming into the 1998 State of Origin series. As happy as Steve was at the Broncos, he had never been able to feel at home at the interstate level. He and Kevvy, despite their reputations at club level, had both struggled in Origin football. Steve was determined to change that.

He went in to the series feeling optimistic. For a start Wayne Bennett was the Queensland coach. 'Steve Renouf was one of the reasons I went back and coached State of Origin,' Bennett explains. 'He was never at his best there because they never treated him properly. He got so much criticism every other year. Criticism never helped Steve Renouf. He never felt they cared because they never showed that.'

Feeling better about the whole process, Steve played well in each of the three matches. In one of the great Origin contests, the Maroons won the first match at Suncorp Stadium 24–23. The Blues came back hard in Sydney to win 26–10.

The tight series was exactly what the code needed. It did a lot to help restore faith in rugby league. There was enormous interest in the decider at Suncorp. It was like the old days: people made their plans for the night. Could the Maroons pull it off?

Injuries and suspensions had put a few holes in the New South Wales line-up. The game had the typical rugged opening. There were few chances. At one stage Steve found himself at dummy half on the left. He actually got a reasonable pass away and it went through the hands to an overlap up the right. It came to Kevvy, of all people, out wide, who took off at Kevvy-pace looking like a man carrying too many grocery bags. But he dummied and was as surprised as anyone to see daylight. So he showed the ball again. And they just kept standing off him. He pinned his ears back and headed for the line. Kevvy Walters running freely – like a possum on a lino floor. Walters: over for a try. It was an important moment in his career.

But the game still had to be won. The Queensland pack was strong. The whole side put in a terrific defensive effort. Steve's long-term battle with Terry Hill continued, and just as the bustling centre looked certain to score Steve barrelled him into the corner post. 'Great strength from Renouf,' came the compliment from commentator Wally Lewis.

Still it was anyone's game. Both packs were clinging on. Gorden Tallis made a half-break and gave a short off-load to Ben Ikin who hit the pass with perfect timing. As he sprinted away he put his fist in the air and put the ball down under the posts.

Steve had a strong game in both attack and defence. It wasn't a flashy performance like the 1997 Grand Final had been, but it was a very satisfying performance, and a satisfying series. Queensland won the decider 19–4, and Steve was so overcome by the feeling that he had overcome his Origin hoodoo that he shed a few tears.

He wasn't the only one feeling a little overwhelmed by it all. No one was going to shut Kevvy Walters up. He was all smiles into the camera, with his balding mate, Alf, behind him. Kevvy was looking older himself. 'I've waited a long time for this,' he said, beaming. 'It just opened up for me. The line wouldn't come quick enough. I think Wayne Bennett's even talking to the media tonight. It's great to be a Queenslander.'

Steve also savoured the moment, and then later announced his retirement from representative football. He was pleased to be going out on a high.

Yet again the Broncos had struggled during the State of Origin period, losing four matches in five weeks, and yet again they stormed home, undefeated in the last eleven rounds to finish minor premiers. They lost the first final to Parramatta 15–10 but then knocked over Melbourne Storm and Sydney City before thrashing Canterbury 38–12 to take the 1998 premiership. They just had too much talent.

Steve was part of a very good football side.

CHAPTER 12

A Sad End and a New Adventure

A T THE BRONCOS' launch for the 1999 season no one could have anticipated the tumult that lay ahead. As revellers sipped away on their beers, everything looked rosy. The Broncos had a chance to show that they were one of the best teams in the recent history of the game by winning a third successive premiership. They had a happy balance. The experienced players – Langer, Walters, Renouf, Hancock, Plath and Gee – were far from being over the hill. And some fine young stars were emerging: Lockyer, Devere, Carroll, Civoniceva and Sailor. Webcke and Tallis were at the height of their powers. The squad was the envy of many coaches.

Steve was happy to just keep doing his bit. He was in the last year of his Super League contract and had become very used to the tidy sum he was earning. If you can talk about football in terms of a market, which those close to the game now tend to do, he was earning what he was worth. He was still what psychologist Phil Jauncey calls 'the spark' at the Broncos. He had won them many games and had helped keep the turnstiles clicking. Other clubs would have paid good money for him but he had always resisted their offers.

The Renouf family were settled and very happy in their newly renovated home at Samford. The kids were getting older. Sam was off to school. Billy was a fearless four-year-old. Sunny was nearly three. And in May of 1999 little Charlie Steven was born. The kids loved the yard and the paddocks, which Lis was slowly filling with the animals she adored. In many ways, Steve and Lis had secured the life they'd dreamt of. Steve was never blasé about it; he was always thankful. He felt blessed.

Lis loved being a mum and Steve loved being a dad. Steve didn't talk about football at home, or watch football. In fact, apart from his aches and pains and his frantic searches for his footy gear on Sundays, there weren't many signs of what he did for a living. But he was away a lot.

Steve was not without his concerns. Lis says he would sometimes worry about the long-term impact of diabetes on his health. He also struggled with the idea of life after football, and although they were in a strong financial position he still wondered how he was going to support his growing clan in the lifestyle they knew. But there were plenty of years left at the Broncos, he thought.

The season started quite bizarrely. The all-conquering Broncos couldn't get a result. They lost a series of close games until eventually they beat Souths. They'd won just one out of six when they went to Townsville and in a tight match scrambled to a come-from-behind draw. And then something remarkable happened. Alf retired. Everyone was bewildered as to why this champion footballer was walking away from the game, Steve included. Why?

Of course this incident generated enormous media coverage in Queensland. And people started talking. Many felt there was more to the story: that there had been a cover-up of some sort, or some kind of falling out. In one media conference Alf looked very sad, and he sounded depressed. It was hard to watch a great character – one of Queensland's favourite sons – go out in such a way. But, for whatever reason, that's what happened, and life went on.

Two more losses followed for the Broncos. They had just three points from nine games.

The players knew they'd have to win pretty well all of the remaining games in order to make the finals – and they started doing just that. Having won four in a row, they took on the Panthers, who were travelling well under coach Royce Simmons, at Penrith. With the game in the balance, Steve took things into his own hands. He beat John Cross and Craig Gower, both handy on their feet, and then with a single step turned three more defenders inside out, sprinted away and dived across the line in an opponent's tackle.

David Potter, reporting for the News Ltd papers, wrote: 'It was vintage Pearl – a try only Brisbane centre Steve Renouf could have created – that spurred the Broncos to their fifth consecutive win.' Royce Simmons was full of praise for the Brisbane centre. 'He's a champion,' he acknowledged. 'And it took a champion try to beat us.'

Steve had another tremendous game against Balmain, scoring two tries, but he injured the ligaments in his ankle quite seriously while chasing down his own grubber kick. Brisbane won again and were well on the way to eleven in a row.

It was during Steve's weeks on the sidelines that negotiations over his contract for the following year gained momentum. Discussions started promisingly. Initially Steve was left with the strong impression the Broncos would do everything they could to keep him. 'I was told that the club owed the senior players for all they had done for the Broncos over the years,' Steve recalls. 'I talked about it with Shane Edwards and we agreed to

a contract. But then that was dropped. Within a matter of a fortnight everything had changed and the message was that the club
owed you nothing. Obviously there was pressure from somewhere, although anyone close to the club knows it is Wayne
Bennett who ultimately makes the decisions at the Broncos.'

Steve grew quite concerned. He had just turned 29 and was
one of the most respected footballers in the world. He realised
that the Broncos were unlikely to re-sign him on the funny money
of his extended Super League contract. That was fair enough.
He was willing to negotiate. He didn't want to go anywhere
else.

The Broncos officials also knew that Steve regarded the Broncos
as his home. They may have gambled on it. They knew the
Renoufs were very settled at Samford. So, in the belief he'd
never leave the Broncos, they offered him a salary of half of his
previous contract.

Steve felt really let down by the offer. He thought it paid little
respect to the contribution he had made, and could still make.
The club had its reasons. 'We were under salary-cap restraint,'
Wayne Bennett explains. 'Pressure was building up. Steve was a
top-class player but his fee, and what he should have been paid,
we couldn't give it to him. He was never going to play for anyone else. He didn't want to play for anyone else. It was impossible
to think of Steve Renouf in another NRL jumper.'

Bennett knew that Steve was upset by the offer. He suggested
to Steve that, if he needed to look elsewhere, he should think
about Leeds. The English clubs were negotiating attractive deals
for Australian players at the end of their careers, and some even
earlier. Wigan had tried to persuade Wendell Sailor to sign for
an amount which would have set him up for life, but he had
decided to stay at the Broncos. Wigan were still keen to find
someone, and Steve let them know that he was available.

It was an unsettling time for Steve – and for Lis. They were unsure of what to do. Steve was hurt by the whole process. He felt betrayed. He had tried for years to take on the values espoused by Wayne Bennett. He had tried so hard to be a young man of substance. But in the heat of the dispute he felt disappointed. He felt that there was a certain hypocrisy in the club. 'There was loyalty when it suited them,' Steve says. At the time, that made him question a lot of what had gone on in the years before.

After agonising over it all, Steve and Lis decided that he should sign with Wigan – for a substantial sum. A couple of his teammates reckon that the Broncos didn't expect that. But he did sign and Family Renouf was off to England. It would take the organisational genius of Lis to effect the planning and execution of the shift.

On 16 July the *Courier-Mail* announced, 'Renouf quits Broncos'. It was front-page news. He was reported to be on a million-dollar contract for two years. 'It's another challenge,' Steve told the newspaper. 'I've done everything I can here. Now it's time for something else.'

The Broncos had some explaining to do to a public that had watched Steve grow from a brilliant but erratic prospect to a champion footballer. They'd watched him become an electrician, get married, and have his family. He was part of their lives – a friend to them. And he had done many sensational things on the footy field. They didn't want to see him go.

Shane Edwards tried to appease the situation, suggesting the Broncos didn't have the money to keep Steve. 'At least he won't be playing against us,' he said in a *Courier-Mail* article.

As if things weren't going badly enough, Steve suffered a serious break to his arm in a game against St George. It meant he had played his last game for the Broncos, finishing without any fanfare, without a chance to say goodbye to the fans.

It's hard to be an injured player around a football club. It's even harder when you know that you're not coming back to that club. He was no longer of any use *whatsoever* to the Broncos, who'd made up sufficient ground in the second half of the season to just sneak into the finals. Steve felt like a real outsider.

His mind was full of questions. Do footballers ever really matter as people? Club administrations always talk about how important players are as people, but do they really care? Or do they just care because the players are useful to them for a short while? Because they can play football? Because they keep the fans coming through the gate? Because they keep the sponsors happy? Because they grease the wheels of business?

These doubts consumed Steve. Had the previous years been for nothing? People mattered to Steve Renouf. And he had come to believe they mattered to the key figures at the Broncos – especially to Wayne Bennett. Steve's faith was being tested.

He didn't say too much. But matters came to a head in the first week of the finals. Steve was still going to training even though he wasn't getting out on the track himself. He still felt he wanted to be there, and to help however he could. He had always been able to travel with the team when he was injured, to be with his team-mates.

At training in the first week of the finals, Steve was told that the club would not cover the costs of his trip to Sydney for the match against Cronulla. He was shattered. 'I felt brushed to the side,' he says. 'Money was not the issue. I had a zillion frequent flyer [points] anyway. It was how it was handled. It was the hypocrisy of it. I felt the qualities Benny had encouraged in me he wasn't upholding himself.'

That weekend Steve found himself letting off steam to his old team-mate Trevor Gillmeister. The steam wafted all the way into 'The Axe's' column in the *Sunday Mail*. Bennett was furious.

The following week Steve was alone in the Broncos dressing room thinking about things when Bennett appeared. 'Wayne had a big go at me,' he recalls, 'about what was in the paper.'

Steve held his ground. 'I've been brushed, have I?' he asked. They argued – forcefully. Bennett turned and left.

Steve was very hurt. He sat in front of his locker, a place he really loved, and shed a tear. This was his place, his home. He had loved being there with his mates, doing what he loved to do. A decade of sitting in the same place. And he was there again, but this time in tears.

As he sat there, Wayne Bennett came out of the team meeting and appeared at the door. He and Steve made eye contact. Bennett turned and walked away. Steve was upset to the core of his being. 'It seemed to be the end of the friendship,' he says.

So this was how it ended at the Broncos. Steve felt the same tearing of flesh he had felt when he left Murgon.

The Broncos lost that final to the Sharks.

At the Broncos Ball a couple of weeks later Steve approached Wayne Bennett and they patched things up. Still, it wasn't supposed to finish the way it did.

Family Renouf treated the move to England as an adventure. The kids were excited about living in another country, and so were their parents. Conventional wisdom suggests that players in the twilight of their career look upon England as some sort of lucrative superannuation scheme, but that's not entirely true. While good money can be made, even for journeymen Australian players, cash is not the only reason for going. Many take the opportunity to experience football in another place, to see how their game is suited to the new situation, how the local way of playing affects their game, and how they perform. Players who have long been restricted by the demands of their yearly routine welcome the opportunity for extended travel and to experience other cultures. Part of the adventure was just to be living in a new place.

The Wigan Warriors Rugby League Football Club made the move very easy for the Renoufs. Everything was organised for them. They got off the plane and virtually walked into their new life: a home, two cars, and assistance with whatever they needed. The kids settled in quickly and were happy. There was so much to see and so much to do. Lis was coping well with the new environment. And for Steve the sadness of leaving the Broncos was in part replaced by an enthusiasm for a fresh start in a new place.

There are lots of similarities between English and Australian life but also some basic differences. Like the weather. And how the place looks. The colours are different. The sky is different. Steve couldn't get over how green everything was, how sometimes it snowed, the accents, and some of the attitudes of the people.

Steve seemed to notice and observe things more readily in England, because they were different, and that encouraged him to reflect not just on life in England but on life in Australia too. At home he had thought things happened just because that was the natural way, but now the cultural differences helped create a sense of perspective.

He became more conscious of overt racism in the community. Issues of race were consistently in the news, and in people's conversation. He noticed the racist comments people made, some jokingly, some bitterly, whereas at home in Australia he had become conditioned to ignore them.

Steve also experienced racism personally a number of times. There were two blatant incidents when Lis was with him. In one he was ignored by a real estate agent, and in the other a shopkeeper made him feel that she wanted nothing to do with him. Lis noticed, and after one of the incidents she asked Steve, 'Is what just happened, what I think just happened?'

Steve wasn't hurt by these incidents, just disappointed that there were those who still treated black people differently. He had experienced it in Australia at times, but it was something he never mentioned to Lis. It seemed more obvious to them in England.

The issue of racism was, in fact, very much in the news in Australia while the Renoufs were in England. Pauline Hanson and the One Nation Party had targeted Aboriginal organisations and the government's immigration policy, advocating her own jaundiced notion of multiculturalism. Steve had not been very interested in politics. He knew of the Mabo and Wik decisions on native title, but he hadn't followed the progress of the reforms closely. But he could see the divisive effect of Pauline Hanson's attitudes, her gross stereotyping, and her limited understanding of cultural difference. She tapped into a latent racism in the community which she exploited for her own political gain. One Nation had won considerable support in country Queensland, in places like Murgon, Gympie and on the Darling Downs. Almost a quarter of Queenslanders voted for One Nation in the state election of 1998, and the party had eleven members in parliament.

Anthony Mundine also helped uncover that deep-seated racism. He had left the Broncos to return to St George where he played a flamboyant, flashy style of rugby league. He believed he should have been a permanent fixture in the New South Wales side, if not the Australian side. He claimed that the selectors were racist, that they were keeping him out of representative football because he was a blackfella.

Anthony Mundine could certainly talk. He called himself 'The Man' and a lot of football fans disliked his compulsion to promote himself, to talk about his own greatness. Some despised him.

But Mundine is a complex character and there is no doubt that he felt, and continues to feel, a deep-seated connection with his people. Consistently he presents himself as something of a modern-day prophet. This brought derision from some and great support from others. He felt a strong obligation to use his profile to highlight the plight of Indigenous Australians, and called on other Aboriginal sportspeople to speak out.

Mundine eventually had had enough of rugby league. He needed time away, so he flew to the United States to be with old friends and consider his future. He arrived at Sydney Airport over a week later, carrying a copy of a Muhammed Ali biography, saying that he had quit rugby league and that he was pursuing a career in the one true sport: boxing.

The media exploited the situation for all it was worth. Large sections of the community laughed at him. Others, especially Indigenous Australians, loved him. To the Aboriginal community he was a hero. Not long after making his debut in the ring he was made NAIDOC Person of the Year.

His actions took immense courage. He walked away from a code where he performed capably and confidently, and was very well-paid, to take up a sport in which he could have been a failure. But Mundine was not short of self-belief. He told everyone that he would win a world title, sooner rather than later, and that, like his hero Muhammed Ali, he would help his people.

Many hoped he would fail. They wished him to fail. In pubs the majority of blokes watching pay-TV coverage of his early fights wanted to see him get his head punched in. There was hatred in their eyes.

Anthony Mundine's story highlights the fact that many Australians just can't see things from an Aboriginal perspective, and some don't have the will to accept difference. They also lack compassion. They have neither the desire nor the capacity to stand in the shoes of another person.

Steve Renouf was aware of these issues. But, while Mundine was willing to tackle them with words, Steve was not a talker. Of course he felt the pain of his people. He was also aware of the opportunity presented to him to help. He was respected by both the Indigenous community and the non-Indigenous community.

Some Aboriginal people thought that Steve wasn't outspoken enough about the plight of his people. But while he was playing football, that wasn't Steve's style. As Chris Johns observes, 'Pearl leads from the front. Pearl shows how you can do things. He's not one to play the 'downtrodden' card. And you wouldn't see him in a riot in Redfern leading the charge . . . Pearl doesn't talk about it. He doesn't need to talk about it. His actions speak.'

A former ATSIC Commissioner from Brisbane, Robbie Williams, says: 'It is very difficult to be a radical black. You've got to be a smart red, black and yellow blackfella, but you can't be over the top.' On the one hand high-profile Aboriginal people feel they want to be a voice on Aboriginal terms; on the other they know that the realpolitik of the situation is: that to be outspoken may alienate sections of the broader community.

While Steve was in England Anthony Mundine was definitely a radical black. He spoke freely. Aboriginal people loved his confidence; they loved that he spoke on their terms. He bolstered their sense of hope.

Steve continued to concentrate on family life and football life. He had little difficulty adjusting to the Wigan routine, and although there wasn't quite the intensity of an NRL campaign, it was all pretty similar. Frank Endecott was the coach of the Warriors at this time.

A football club is rarely a lonely place when you're fit and playing well, and there were plenty of familiar Australian faces around: Matthew Johns, Adrian Lam, Brett Dallas and David Furner were all at Wigan. Other mates were dotted around the country-side: Jason Smith at Hull; Tonie Carroll at Leeds; Mick Hancock at Salford; Allan Langer and Andrew Gee at Warrington.

Steve wasn't really a veteran. He was only turning 30 in that first season, and time hadn't taken much toll on his pace or his skills. In his brief stint at Warrington, Kevin Walters came up against Pearl. He remembers the match: 'I was marking him. It was a nightmare. I was pretty slow and he was pretty quick. He was cutting me up. I managed to get a hold of him once and I whispered, 'Mate, you're going to have to look after me here. I don't mind you making a couple of breaks, but not all day, hey!' He just got up and smiled and winked at me. He made a couple of breaks and then left me alone.'

The boys went back a long way.

In reflecting on things, Steve found himself thinking about his time in rugby league. He had the self-knowledge to realise that he was an unconventional footballer in any club. Sometimes that worried him. Steve remembers ringing Wayne Bennett one day:

I told him I felt bad. I was around footy players and they wanted to talk footy but that I didn't want to. I was thinking that there was something wrong with me . . . I was feeling guilty for not being a footy-head. Wayne reassured me, saying that he respected me for that. He said he wished some other players were a bit more like me, because some of them just can't let go. That's all they've got. But he said, 'I know you've got other things.' It made me feel good again.

But generally, when Steve looked back over his career, he was happy with his football. 'The team actually respected me for being a bit different,' he says. 'Like, I was never in their blokey things. I never went on an end-of-year trip because I preferred to be at home with Lis and the young kids. The guys didn't begrudge me. I used to worry about it a bit. Sometimes I'd get a bit paranoid: "Did I fit in? Was I on the outer?" And there were times when probably I was, but that was alright.'

Wigan made the Grand Final in both seasons Steve was there. They lost the first to St Helens and the second to Bradford.

Playing at the re-developed Old Trafford stadium was one of the highlights of Steve's time in England. It is a place of sporting and social significance, the home of one of the premier sporting clubs of the world, Manchester United. Steve had the same feeling he'd had when he'd played at Wembley. He felt linked with the grand history of the place, honoured to be on the turf where some of the world's finest sportsmen had played in memorable contests before cheering, appreciative crowds.

Towards the end of the second season Family Renouf was very happy. There had been an addition: Freddie, their fifth child, had been born in May. They had had visitors from Australia. Steve's mother even left Palmer Street for a few weeks to visit them in England. In fact things were going so well that they decided to stay. Steve was in negotiations with both Bradford and Widnes when the World Trade Centre tragedy occurred on 11 September 2001. It affected Steve and Lis profoundly.

It was time to come home.

CHAPTER 13

Life after Football

THE RENOUF FAMILY – all seven of them – returned to Australia early in 2002. They were happy to be back at Samford. Lis set about getting the household up and running. Sam, Billy and Sunny went off to school. Charlie and Freddie enjoyed the warm sunshine, the Queensland verandahs and the big yard. For Steve it was a time of uncertainty.

He was giving more and more thought to his career after football. It caused him some consternation whenever it surfaced. But he still had time: he wasn't sure in his own mind whether he had retired from the game or not. He felt that he had good football left in him and he knew that it wouldn't be too hard to flush out any interest that existed from NRL clubs around the country. But, if he were to play, he wanted to play at the Broncos. He talked with Wayne Bennett.

The coach was almost persuaded by Steve's enthusiasm. It was a difficult decision for the club which, if anything, was in need of a game-breaker. Steve was almost 32 and had been out of the Australian game for two and a half years, but he was confident he had plenty to offer the Broncos. 'The hard part was that he wanted to play when he came home,' Bennett recalls, 'and I nearly relented there.' But, Bennett was conscious of the need to continually develop the emerging young talent, to keep re-inventing the Brisbane Broncos.

Steve's moment had passed. He had to accept the fact that, while he would always be part of the club, there was no place for him on the field at the Broncos, and that it was time to move on to a new stage in his life. That's just the way it was.

The uncertainty worried Steve though. Even though football had never been the most important thing in Steve's life, it had occupied so much time and required such endeavour that retirement meant major changes. It had never defined him, but it had had a profound effect on his sense of himself, and on his interaction with people in and out of the football world. He had loved being with his mates at the Broncos: young men who shared the common understanding of what it meant to be a professional footballer, who strived for things together, who trained hard and played together, who lived the highs and lows together, who laughed together.

The realisation that football was finished brought changes, but Steve didn't suffer the deep sense of loss that some footballers do. Bennett acknowledges that it is often heart-wrenching for all concerned, but that professional football is relentless and you can't dwell on the past.

'You don't see them as much as you did,' he says. 'You come to the team meeting and [think] this is where Steve used to sit and this is where Alfie used to sit. They all sat in the same seats. But I've got another Steve Renouf now, and I've got to get him to be the best he can be. I've got to let them go. And that's the hard part because they've been such a part of your life.'

Steve had made many friends through football and had many memories. But like Bennett he knew that he just had to keep those memories while looking to the future. He began looking at the possibilities more intently. Media work held some attraction and he was offered a role on triple M's Saturday morning sports show, *Blood, Sweat and Beers*. Later in the season he was involved in Channel 9's State of Origin coverage.

But he wanted a more definite career: a role in an organisation where he felt he could make a full-time contribution while developing an understanding of, and the skills for, that profession. When an opportunity emerged at Sport and Recreation Queensland, Steve took up a position as a Community Programs Officer, helping to coordinate and lead a new skills program to be made available to all Queensland schools. The department wanted to make use of the abilities of the scholarship holders at the Queensland Academy of Sport (QAS), and to give them experience in teaching and leadership roles. Schools were invited to apply to be involved in a day program where QAS athletes would come to their school or community and take the children through a series of age-specific seminars and clinics to make them more aware of healthy living and physical activity and exercise. The athletes would talk about exercise and diet and sun-safe issues, and then take the kids outside to complete a series of skill-based activities to promote movement, agility and eye–hand coordination. They wanted to help kids realise that being active is fun. Depending on the age of the group, contemporary issues like drugs in sport might also be canvassed.

This program was extremely successful over the three years of Steve's involvement. His role was to organise the athletes' visits to schools, and to encourage and target some schools where the need appeared obvious. He travelled to many places throughout the state, including some of the Aboriginal communities.

Brian Kerle, who works for the department, has also involved Steve in the 'Locker Room' forums which are held throughout

Queensland to promote better values and attitudes in sporting competitions and organisations. Kerle invites some of the most successful people from the Queensland sporting fraternity to speak and then answer questions. Early in Steve's career at Sport and Recreation he spoke about his own experience at a night in Ipswich attended by over 300 people. The line-up included a sagacious Wayne Bennett, former Brisbane Lion Richard Champion, Hockeyroo Nicki Hudson and an energetic and amusing Phil Jauncey.

As Minister for Sport, Terry Mackenroth was delighted when Steve joined the department. A great fan of rugby league, Mr Mackenroth is sometimes called the Minister for the Broncos. He followed Steve's playing career closely and rates Steve and Mal Meninga as the finest centres in the modern era. These days he can see the qualities Steve brings to his work in public administration. 'He's recognised everywhere. There's no doubt about that. He remains very well-known and loved throughout Queensland,' Mr Mackenroth says. 'He is an ambassador for sport and a role model for all Queenslanders.' The minister is keen to see Steve develop his skills in government, and can see the impact he is having in the community.

Steve has now moved into a new job in the Queensland Government's Office of Economic and Statistical Research, a unit that gathers data about the state. Steve's role is to develop a strategy to encourage Aboriginal Queenslanders to participate in Census 2006 next August. He is coordinating a marketing and information campaign to help make people living in Indigenous communities aware of the benefits of completing the census forms. This is an important challenge, as federal and state government funds tend to be distributed according to the official figures, and in many communities there are more people than the census information suggests. There are ramifications for many social services: health, education, housing and other infrastructure.

Since returning from England Steve has been called on by many community organisations. He promotes the Salvation Army Christmas Toy Appeal and works as an ambassador for Queensland Rail on iniatives like their Christmas Appeal. He has been the face of an Indigenous employment scheme whereby he spoke to business people in regional cities and towns, encouraging them to place Aboriginal people in jobs. He featured in a television ad for the scheme and also appears on their informative literature.

Numerous government organisations have asked him to support their programs, such as the anti-bullying program and the program which encourages young people to remain in schools.

Steve is often invited to speak and present the awards at end-of-season functions for clubs and schools. He is especially popular in regional schools, where his simple message is to get involved and enjoy what you're doing and to believe that you can come from the bush and be successful in sport or any endeavour. To encourage participation in rugby league, the Steve Renouf Shield, a school-based Year 8 competition, has been instituted. Steve presents the trophy each year.

He has had roles in a range of cultural events. He was pleased to head back to Murgon for the arts festival. A prize has been named in his honour: the Steve Renouf Indigenous Arts Award. He was also part of the centenary celebrations at Murgon, during which the community put together a choreographed spectacular telling the history of the district. It involved many local people, some of whom returned – like Leah Purcell – for the extravaganza. Steve loved the commentary of the mock football game between the Under 10s of Murgon and Cherbourg. Steve was happy to be back in Murgon, celebrating his home town. On another visit he was inducted into the Murgon Hall of Fame, a night when a painting of him as a footballer was unveiled.

Of special significance to Steve is his work with the diabetes organisations. Over the last few years, three of the Renouf children – Billy, Charlie and Freddie – have been diagnosed with diabetes. They deal with the intrusive condition very stoically, as does their dad.

Steve is determined to do what he can to help build public awareness of diabetes and raise much-needed funds in the hope of finding a cure for the disorder. The peak national body, Diabetes Australia, often uses Steve in its campaigns. He has been MC at the Walk for the Cure launch, and, at a function in Sydney on World Diabetes Day, he handed over the cheques to doctors and scientists involved in research. Steve is also one of the faces of the 'Great Australian Bite' campaign, which is the organisation's most recent initiative. The advertising campaign includes an image of Steve playing football and the caption, 'Steve Renouf, former rugby league great says: Let's tackle diabetes by hosting a "bite".' People are encouraged to get together with friends for a meal and then make a contribution to diabetes research.

The management of diabetes is an ever-present issue for the Renouf family. The three boys are very good with their testing. But Steve and Lis are always looking at ways of improving the management strategy and technique. To this end, based on their own personal experience, they have developed a range of prod-ucts and a record-keeping system, with supporting literature, to make the management of diabetes easier. They have formed a company to manufacture and distribute the products. This is an exciting new part of the family's life.

The Renoufs lead an active life, with Steve's work and role in the community and the kids involved at school and in their sporting clubs and doing other activities. Sam and Billy play football at the Samford Stags. Lis has her work cut out coordinating everything.

But in 2004 the household's schedule became even busier when Steve decided he wanted to return to football. Halfway through the season, former Broncos team-mate Darren Smith, looking to bolster his side, asked Steve to come and play with him at Easts. Steve had remained active, training in the Broncos gym from time to time (some say harder than when he played at the Broncos). He enjoyed the exercise and he enjoyed being in the dressing sheds and sitting at his old locker. So it wasn't going to take much to get in fair enough shape to play in the Queensland Cup competition.

Some were surprised by the decision. But it was easy for Steve. It wasn't as if he was dissatisfied with life after football and desperately needed to be part of it again. He wanted to help out an old team-mate, and he just wanted to play football again, to get out on the paddock and enjoy himself.

Easts were pleased to have him. There was a lot of public interest in his comeback and Langlands Park was packed with a crowd of around 4,000 for his return match. It was the biggest crowd seen there for a long time. Terry Mackenroth, number one ticket holder at Easts, says the people had come to see Steve. Some thought he might be contemplating a return to the NRL.

Although not as quick as he had been, he was still a class act. He still moved well and hadn't lost that knack for scoring tries, and despite a few weeks on the sidelines with niggly injuries, he helped Easts into the finals. In the preliminary final against Wynnum, he scored three times.

At Suncorp Stadium a big crowd watched one of the best local grand finals for a long time. The Burleigh Bears led at half-time, but a try from Steve got the Tigers within striking distance. With minutes to go, and still down by six points, they were attacking when Steve broke his arm, the same bone that he had broken in 1999. He trudged off. Darren Smith, on one leg, rallied his charges and in the dying seconds Easts winger Steve Beattie scored. Dane Campbell converted from the touchline to level the scores. The golden point rule was in place and Steve watched from the sidelines, arm in a makeshift sling, as tired footballers battled it out, end to end, in a superb contest that went for nineteen minutes before Shane O'Flanagan scored to give Burleigh the premiership.

That was it for football.

Playing for Easts was more like playing back in Murgon. Steve was like an amateur again, and football was extracurricular to his family life and work life. Indeed, being out of the professional game since returning from England gave Steve a different focus. He had more time to reflect on things which he previously took for granted.

He looked back on his life. It had changed significantly in 1988 when he first moved from Murgon to Brisbane in an attempt to make it in professional rugby league. Although the decision was difficult, he found he was willing to push aspects of his identity to the side, for the sake of a football career. Wayne Bennett said it was the only way he could do it. But the coach also knew that it was temporary. 'Steve lost himself for a decade to be a professional footballer, and being a professional footballer is one of his greatest achievements,' Bennett concludes. 'But he never really lost himself. The Aboriginal part of him is coming back because he's not in that [football] environment anymore.'

Identity runs very deeply in all of us. Steve will always be a footballer. He will always have that football experience in him. But there are other dimensions to his identity. You can't have the family heritage that Steve has, and the rich experiences of childhood, without it having a profound effect on who you really are. When Steve approached me to help him write his story, initially I was to be the technician who got the words down. But it became clear that Steve wanted to use the process of producing the book not only to tell his story in and out of football but also to explore and think about his life and his heritage. Hence the book became more of a researched biography, as well as being the story Steve has told.

Increasingly over the last couple of years Steve has felt the sense of his Aboriginality emerging, and a need to understand the past which forms the foundation of that identity. He also wants his own children to have a sense of themselves as Aboriginal Australians.

Steve Renouf grew up in an Aboriginal home in country Queensland. He was immersed in the culture of that home. He developed a particular way of understanding the world – whether he was conscious of it or not. He was taken to the bush by Old Charlie and his uncles. Although he experienced something of the traditional way, he largely enjoyed a contemporary Aboriginal life. During his time in professional football he was away from those elements of his background.

Occasionally, during his years in football, Steve was disappointed when comments were made that football and the Broncos somehow 'rescued' him from Murgon and his past. That discourse of rescue frustrated Steve because it implicitly disregarded where Steve had come from. Steve Renouf wasn't rescued. There was nothing to be rescued from. He came from a rich and satisfying culture, and was proud of that culture.

These days Steve's sense of Aboriginality, and what it symbolises, beats within him. It always has; it is just more immediate now. His children also have a sense of their Aboriginality and Steve wants to give them an opportunity to explore that more.

Steve himself doesn't have a strong traditional cultural knowledge, but he does have a strong sense of himself as an Aboriginal person and a strong need to find out what that means to him. So, as is his way, he seeks out people who understand him and have that cultural knowledge, to talk with him, advise him and help him. Elissa is, of course, completely supportive of this.

One of the people that Steve has turned to is Frankie Malone, with whom he has strong cultural and family bonds. As well as their Aboriginal heritage and close family connection, Frankie and Steve also have the shared experience of a sporting gift, a rugby league gift. Both have in them a rare talent. They know they have it, yet find it difficult to explain. It is an unspoken link that makes them very close.

Steve and Lis and the kids love going to the bush with Frankie, and they go whenever they can, usually at Easter, along with other family members. One year they went camping between Murgon and Gayndah at Barambah Gorge with four of Steve's sisters and their families. So there were stacks of kids. Frankie took them out collecting (and eating) witchetty grubs which were relatively easy to find. He helped them to make spears which the kids were determined to use to catch a goanna.

For a couple of days (whenever they remembered) the kids were on the lookout for a goanna in the bush. But it was too hilly and too thick with scrub and, although they could hear the rustling as they walked, they didn't spot one. The kids were getting a bit dejected. Then, as they walked along the creek, they came across a big one. The kids were instantly focused, alert with the possibility of goanna for dinner. Hearing the commotion, Frankie raced down from the campsite and managed to stun the big creature. As he did, the kids came from everywhere and speared it. Frankie was dancing around. The kids were thrilled.

As they walked back to the campsite to cook up their catch, Lis told Frankie that he looked like a real Aborigine when he was dancing around the goanna. Frankie put his arm around her and said, 'I am an Aborigine.'

The kids loved it. They dug a hole, made a fire and covered the goanna with coals. And when it was cooked they sat around together and ate it. It tasted like chicken.

Although Steve's sense of himself is not dependent on engaging with the traditional ways, it is a heritage he respects, and it somehow allows the focus to fall on the aspects of their Aboriginal heritage. The further Steve goes, the more he feels that sense of himself, and the more he feels that he wants to find a way to contribute to the Aboriginal community.

Unlike Anthony Mundine, Steve Renouf has not had much to say about these matters over the years. Steve will only speak when he feels he is ready to speak. He is patient. And, at the moment, he is formulating his position on how best he can help his people. He is observing and listening. There are some things he doesn't like about sections of the Aboriginal leadership. There are things he sees as valuable. But he is still coming to an understanding of the issues.

There are many who believe he will one day make a more overt contribution. And Steve himself is feeling more and more that he would like to do it. After the Palm Island tragedy he said, 'I just felt so frustrated about it all. I felt like going up there and seeing what I could do.'

Wayne Bennett believes that Steve will find his place. 'I've always encouraged Steve to go back and work with Aboriginal people. He's a class act. He [fits in] in any company. He makes sense. And he cares. So my encouragement has always been to go back and become a leader amongst his people. I've got no doubt that will happen down the track. It's a case of finding the right place – where he can make a contribution. It's not just a case of getting a job in that environment. He's made his own way. He's made his own career. He's stood on his own feet.'

The time will come.

Conclusion

S TEVE RENOUF WAS a magnificent footballer. He gave us many memories. He moved with such grace and beauty. And pace. No one ever knew how fast The Pearl was. He didn't himself. He always said that he was 'fast enough'. He played instinctively. He just played the game as it unfolded in front of him. Often, as he approached the defence, he had no idea of what he was about to do, or why things happened the way they did.

That's one of the reasons he appealed so much. His brilliance and the intuitive nature of his performance made us feel that there was something more, something greater into which we are occasionally allowed to glimpse. Roy Masters, the elder statesman of rugby league scribes, once wrote, 'When Steve Renouf takes the ball and surges forward you sense that this is how God wants football to be played.'

Yet Steve always distanced himself from his own talent. In his mind, it was a natural gift, for which he was thankful.

His success made people interested in who he was. Bucko: this quiet, unassuming Aboriginal bloke from Murgon who has always been his own man. Never the man others thought he should be, just the man he is. He has never allowed the past to prescribe or determine the future, nor does he dismiss its impact.

Steve Renouf has shown that it is important to understand that people come from different backgrounds and have different understandings of the world, and that ways can be found so that everyone feels that their interests have been taken into consideration.

He has also shown that struggle is just part of life, and while sometimes they are individual and solitary struggles, at other times they are struggles that can be tackled with the cooperation of others. With the unfailing love, encouragement and drive of Lis, the faith and trust of Wayne Bennett, and the support of his team-mates, he fought to overcome the self-doubt which, despite his natural ability, threatened to keep him from the professional football field. And he *did* overcome it.

So too there is struggle in everyday life, especially for Aboriginal people, who live with the collective memory of a past shattered by colonial attitudes, and with the residue of racism that remains. Issues of identity are ever-present. Sometimes they are hidden away, and then surface in complex ways.

Steve is finding his own understanding of things. Family means so much to Steve: Old Charlie, Mum Nerida, Nan South, his brothers and sisters, his other relatives. And now, of course, Lis, and their own children who fill their home with energy and laughter.

The sense of place means much to him as well: their own home now, his locker at the Broncos, and Murgon. Cold Chisel's song 'Flame Trees' is one of his favourites because it reminds him so much of Murgon. 'We shared some history, this town and I . . . And I'm wondering if he'll go or if he'll stay/Do you remember, nothing stopped us on the field in our day.'

Murgon is Steve's country. It's where his football started. It's where he met Lis. It's also where the prejudice of the narrow-minded put pressure on their young relationship and where they showed that they would not be deterred and that they would fight for their love.

Racist prejudices upset Steve, as they do many Australians. He would love to do what he can to extinguish such attitudes. A few years ago Aunty Ruth Hegarty, an Indigenous relative of Steve's who grew up at Cherbourg, made a memorable statement. Speaking at the 'Bringing them Home' reception in front of 5,000 people in King George Square, when Lord Mayor Jim Soorley officially welcomed the Aboriginal community back into the centre of Brisbane, she said, 'I look forward to the day when we are all Indigenous Australians.' It's a view that Steve shares – that we can all think of Australia as home no matter what our heritage.

Steve is now in a position to have an influence. Football brought Steve to the attention of the community. People will remember The Pearl in full flight for a long time. Football has won him a public profile, and he continues to show he is a young man of character. He wants to use that profile to help the community.

The challenge for Steve now is to find the best way of doing that.

Acknowledgments

A lot of people have helped in the process of writing this book.

I wish to thank Bill Walker who suggested to Steve that I write his story; Laurie Muller, then the general manager at UQP, who was enthusiastic about the project from the start and has offered wise counsel throughout; Wayne Coolwell for his knowledge, understanding, encouragement and insight; and Jackie Huggins for her support and advice.

Thank you to Arts Queensland for the grant which kicked off the research and the writing.

Of course, thanks go to Steve and Elissa Renouf for telling me their story. Also to Mrs Nerida Renouf, Charlie Renouf, Debbie Renouf, Paul and Colleen Bishop, Sonia Renouf, Steve Button, Frankie Malone, Cliff Douglas, Kerry Renouf, Bruce and Jenny Bishop, Clinton Weier, Greg and Carmel Smith, Sue Monson, Nicole Rangier, Paul Richards, Matt Foley, Brian Hodgson, John Hunter, Wayne Bennett, Tony Durkin, Ray Herring, Phil Jauncey, Tony Currie, Chris Johns, Kevin Walters, Andrew Johns, Rod Kilner, Robbie Williams, Herb Bligh and Terry Mackenroth, and to the many who have taken time to chat informally about Steve Renouf.

A special thanks to Glenda Tanner, a cousin of Steve's, who was a tremendous help in piecing together the Renouf family heritage.

Thanks to those who have taken time to read and comment on sections of the manuscript: Peter and David Harms, Paul Daffey, Martin Flanagan, and especially Michael Harms and Anthony W. Collins.

Thanks to Steele Taylor for the photograph of the Murgon grandstand. Thanks to the staff of the Fryer Library at the University of Queensland, the National Archives of Australia and the Australian War Memorial.

Thanks to historians Dr Ken Edwards and Dr Murray Phillips, newspaper editors Peter Hanlon and Warwick Green, and Lion Nathan for permission to reprint the words from a 1991 advertisement.

Thanks to my editor, Felicity McKenzie, and to Greg Bain, Rob Cullinan, Ben Robertson and Eliza Kennedy at UQP. Thanks to Madonna Duffy for her understanding.

Finally, thanks to Susan, a world expert on persistence.

I would like to acknowledge the following authors: Jack Gallaway (*The Brisbane Broncos: The Team to Beat* and *Origin: Rugby League's Greatest Contest 1980–2002*), Wayne Bennett (*Don't Die with the Music in You*), Mike Colman and Ken Edwards (*Eddie Gilbert*), Thom Blake (*A Dumping Ground*), Anthony Mundine (*The Man*), Mike Colman (*Super League: The Inside Story*), and the videos *Broncos – Born to Win!* and *Back to Back*.